T0165034

LIVIA'S LEGACY

By Dagmar Wirch

Order this book online at www.trafford.com
or email orders@trafford.com

Most Trafford titles are also available at major online book retailers.

© Copyright 2012 Dagmar Wirch.
All rights reserved. No part of this publication may be reproduced, stored in a retrieval system, or transmitted, in any form or by any means, electronic, mechanical, photocopying, recording, or otherwise, without the written prior permission of the author.

Printed in the United States of America.

ISBN: 978-1-4269-9243-8 (sc)
ISBN: 978-1-4269-9244-5 (hc)
ISBN: 978-1-4269-9245-2 (e)

Library of Congress Control Number: 2011914531

Trafford rev. 01/25/2012

 www.trafford.com

North America & international
toll-free: 1 888 232 4444 (USA & Canada)
phone: 250 383 6864 ♦ fax: 812 355 4082

PREFACE TO LIVIA'S LEGACY

Writing this book has been an intellectual and emotional challenge. As I tried to relive the experiences through my mother's perspective, I was often moved to tears. After reviewing her incredible courage and faith, I am proud to be Livia's offspring.

In order to be historically accurate, I gathered facts from the public domain of internet sites, eg: "The Lodz Ghetto", "Holocaust Encyclopedia", "Born from Ashes and Blood, Poland in World War II", by Laura Knight Jadczyk, "To the Lodz Station", by Andrew Jakabowicz and "Bombing Dresden In World War II". I also drew bits of information from James Michener's book, "Poland" and from a German book about Germans in Lodz.

Much of the information in Part I is based upon a memoir, hand-written in German, by my deceased Aunt Lydia, Livia's sister. As a young child, I was fascinated when these stories were told. Later on in life, I knew that I had to pass them on. Because many details or records were unavailable, I had to rely on my memory and imagination to reconstruct the events. The events in Part II are recorded as well as I remember them, with a few flights of fancy. Except for the names of close relatives, other names have been changed to protect the identities of those individuals. Any personal reference is unintentional.

I want to express my sincere appreciation to my husband, Arthur, for his support, patience and help in bringing this book to publication.

I would like to dedicate my book to my brother Frank and my sister Margot.

PART I

TREK INTO THE UNKNOWN

CHAPTER 1

Anxiety clouded Livia's vision, as she elbowed her way through the crowd at the main railway station in Lodz, Poland. She was dressed in a beige raincoat and a silk scarf covered her dark brown hair. Loud voices echoed around her like waves on a stormy sea. Clutching her handbag and umbrella, she ignored muttered curses on her way to the ticket counter. At last, with her ticket in hand, she leaned against a pillar and gazed around the cavernous hall.

Her eyes were drawn to the only bright spot in the dingy surroundings. Hanging on the wall was a blood-red flag with a black swastika in bold relief against the central white circle.

Livia shuddered and turned away from the Nazi symbol. Wartime was a bad time for her trip to *Posen*. 'No matter what is happening, I must get to the *Posen* Children's Hospital to see my little girl,' thought Livia.

Just then, a tremendous clanging and hissing reverberated through the hall as the train steamed into the station. Livia joined the long queue snaking towards the boarding gate. A military policeman, wearing a swastika armband, stopped her progress. "Open your bag," he demanded brusquely. She snapped it open for his inspection. "Where are you going?"

"To *Posen*," answered Livia softly.

"Speak up!" he barked, "And what is your business there?"

"I want to visit my baby daughter in the Children's Hospital," answered Livia. The guard checked her identification papers. "Be on you way, then," he grumbled. "Next, please."

Heaving a sigh of relief, Livia stepped onto the platform. Her eyes stung from the oppressive smoke hanging in the air. Quickly, she grabbed a hold of the handrail and heaved herself up into the waiting passenger car. She found an empty seat on the wooden bench, near a window. In a few minutes, the conductor shouted, "All aboard!" The train began to chug from the station.

Heavy showers streamed from the leaden sky. Through the rain-streaked window, Livia saw the tall chimneys of the textile factories rushing past. Soon, the residential districts were also left far behind. Billowing clouds of black smoke, the train chugged out of *Litzmannstadt*, which was the new German name for the old city of Lodz.

Livia's mood was as gray as the weather. What had happened to her beloved home of Poland? So much had changed since her German ancestors had settled here. Once, they lived peacefully together with their Polish neighbors, but now . . . Ever since Hitler's armies had invaded Poland on September 1, 1939, the Nazis had been stirring up trouble. The *Fuehrer's* propaganda told everyone that the Germans would win the war. But . . . Livia wondered what the future really held.

She glanced nervously around at her fellow passengers. Could they read her thoughts? The wooden seats were packed. Across from Livia, an elderly man hid behind a German Newspaper. HITLER DEMANDS MORE *LEBENSRAUM* FOR GERMANS the headline screamed. Beside the old man, a young *Brownshirt* dozed, swaying back and forth with the movement of the train. He was probably on his way to join his troupe in *Posen*. From the other side, came the pungent smell of garlic. A middle-aged, Polish peasant woman sat there, clad in a colorful kerchief and long apron over her full skirt. She clutched a large covered basket on her lap. A young, runny-nosed boy leaned against her ample shoulders. She briefly glanced at Livia with large frightened eyes. The other passengers looked like statues with vacant expressions.

Livia's thoughts turned from them to the reason for her trip – Dagmar. 'My darling child, so far away from me,' she thought. 'I am on my way. Soon, I will see you again, *mein Liebling.*' This fragile child had been her answer to prayer after Marlene's death. Sweet little Marlene, who had succumbed to diphtheria, had been the family's darling. Oh, the agony Livia had suffered after her first daughter's death! Her nerves were still raw. Now, her precious replacement daughter was so ill. Livia's arms ached to hold six month-old Dagmar again, to never let her go.

Time seemed to stand still as the sodden landscape whizzed past. It usually took two hours from *Litzmanstadt* to *Posen*, but today it seemed to take forever. Hunger pangs began to gnaw. This morning, Livia had been unable to eat anything. She was glad that she had packed a sandwich of dark rye bread spread with liverwurst and a thermos of coffee. After munching on her sandwich and sipping her coffee, she began to feel better. She cleaned away the crumbs and leaned back against the wooden seat. Her eyes closed as she dozed off. Suddenly, she jerked awake. "Next stop, *Posen*," the conductor shouted across the compartment.

A tumult of bodies engulfed her outside the station. She raised her umbrella, dodged past the throng of people and splashed across the cobblestone market. On a sunny day, she would have admired the graceful architecture of the old burgher houses that lined the square. Today, every façade was drab and wet. Livia hurried along, trying to avoid the puddles. Straight ahead, loomed the gray, brick Children's Hospital. Livia's footsteps quickened.

Suddenly, a little black dog darted out of an alley, started barking and nipping at her heels. Livia kicked him aside. Nothing slowed her down. She dashed up the hospital steps. How was her little daughter?

All hospital visits were regulated by strict Nazi administration rules. Livia knew that she must first register at the main desk and obtain official permission to visit the isolation ward.

Just then, she heard a child crying far away down the hall. She listened. It could not be – it was – yes, it was Dagmar's voice! Livia forgot all about the rules, as she flew down the hall to her daughter's room. She pushed the door open. There was her baby, sobbing in her crib.

Without thinking, Livia scooped up the child. "Sh—sh-sh, *Liebling*, Mommy is here, don't cry, *Liebling*," she crooned into her daughter's ear. The child's eyes flew open in amazement. Gradually, her sobs began to subside. The baby sighed loudly and clung to her mother. Livia's eyes examined the beloved little face. She saw that Dagmar's skin infection was not completely healed. Bright red spots and scabs still covered her baby's skin. After two weeks in this hospital, the condition should have improved. These Nazi doctors could not be trusted. What kind of medicine were they giving to the child? Maybe it was the wrong kind – just like Marlene's case. And why was Dagmar left alone when she was crying?

Livia's grip tightened around her baby. This time, she would not allow the doctors to experiment on her child. Old-fashioned herbal salves, like her father had used, would work much better. At home, her child would never be neglected.

"What are you doing in here?" a male voice boomed behind Livia. She jumped around, with Dagmar in her arms, to face a stern-looking doctor.

"I am Livia Falk, Dagmar's mother," she stammered.

"*Frau* Falk, I must ask you to leave immediately," the doctor ordered. "Your daughter is in isolation. No one is allowed to enter without protective, sterile clothing. I can hardly imagine how many germs you brought in here. Please return to the desk at once for proper protective garments."

"I cannot leave my child right now," replied Livia. "She will start crying again." The mother stared defiantly at the doctor.

"You must conform to hospital regulations, *Frau* Falk," said the doctor. "Your daughter will be fine until you return."

Livia's heart was pounding as she held her daughter in a tight embrace. Right then and there she made up her mind. "*Herr Doktor*, I am not leaving my daughter now, or ever. I am taking her home with me today." She spoke firmly, even though her knees were shaking.

"*Frau* Falk, please be reasonable. I cannot permit you to take Dagmar home. She is not fully recovered. The consequences could be tragic." The doctor warned. "I refuse to sign the discharge papers."

"Then, I will take full responsibility for her myself," answered Livia. "I am taking my child home with or without your permission."

"You are out of your mind, *Frau* Falk," the doctor shouted over his shoulder as he stormed out of the room.

"*Liebling*, we are going home," Livia crooned into her baby's ear. "Please don't cry anymore while I get you dressed." Quickly, she pulled Dagmar's clothing from the wardrobe. As she dressed the child, Livia noticed that it was still raining outside. "I will have to wrap you in one of the hospital blankets," she said to her child. Before leaving the room, Livia placed two *Reichsmark* into the crib. The money would be enough to pay for the blanket.

In a few minutes, the young mother walked down the hallway carrying her tightly wrapped bundle over her left shoulder and clutching her handbag and umbrella in her right hand. Would she make it past the main desk? "Halt! *Frau* Falk!" someone shouted, but Livia was already at the exit. She pushed the heavy door open with all her might and nearly fell down the steps. She raised her umbrella and started to run down the wet street, but then, forced herself to slow down.

"I must walk normally, as though nothing is wrong," she said to herself. She decided to take a detour down narrow side streets. Was anyone following her? Livia did not dare to glance back. Instead, she zigzagged back to the main street. Through the drizzle, she saw a troupe of soldiers goose-stepping toward her. Were they going to arrest her? She squeezed herself and her bundle into the recess of a doorway. The troupe marched past, raising their hands in a salute and shouting, *"Heil Hitler!"* Livia mumbled a reply as she hurried toward the train station.

Panting from the exertion, she entered the huge building. Gratefully, she sank onto a wooden bench and turned her back to the entrance. "Please, Lord, let us get home safely," she prayed.

The waiting period seemed endless. After a while, Livia had recovered enough to purchase a small bottle of milk for Dagmar and a poppy seed roll for her self. The baby slurped the milk and fell asleep in her mother's arms while Livia munched on her own treat.

Half an hour later, the clanging train thundered into the station. Dagmar woke suddenly and let out a loud wail from her cocoon. "Sh-sh-sh, *Liebling, Sei still,*" her mother soothed, rocking the child. There was no time to waste. Livia had to board the train. As her mother hurried to the gate, the child stopped crying. How glad Livia was that there was no guard on duty this time! She found a seat in the farthest corner of the compartment for herself and her precious bundle. When the conductor came to punch her ticket, she didn't have to pay extra for her under-age child. Several other people boarded the train. Livia kept her darling tightly wrapped, leaving only a small opening. She looked out the window, ignoring curious stares.

Dagmar squirmed for a while, but was rocked to sleep with the movement of the train. With every breath, the mother prayed for her *Liebling's* complete recovery.

The flat countryside whizzed past in a gray blur. Livia willed the train to go faster as she thought of home. 'What will I tell Eduard?' she mused. She hoped that her husband was taking proper care of young Frank. It would not be the first time that the boy got neglected while his father was off in his own world. Probably, Eduard would be preparing his sermon for Sunday. If only he could stick to his topic instead of rambling on. Livia was certain that the congregation was keeping him out of pity for his weak, physical condition. She shook herself as she tried to take her mind off this painful topic. Somehow, she would make everything work out when she got home.

At last, the train chugged into the main station at *Litzmannstadt*. Livia's eyes searched the platform. She spotted Eduard's tall, thin form. He was waving his hat. Beside him, Frank was craning his neck, trying to see past taller people. Livia and her bundle were jostled along until she reached her husband and son. Frank tore away from his father and threw his arms around his mother's knees. She almost lost her balance.

"Mommy, I am so glad you are back," he shouted. "Did you bring me anything?"

"Don't knock me over, please," replied Livia. "I am happy to be back, too. Yes. I brought you something special – your sister."

"You did what?" Eduard asked. Meanwhile, Frank bounced up and down like a ball.

"Dagmar is home!" he yelled.

"Be quiet, Frank," his father said sternly. "Everyone can hear you. You will see your sister soon enough. Come, let us take the streetcar home." Once the family was settled on the tram,

Eduard wanted to see his daughter. "She still looks sick," he said. "Did the doctor give you permission to take her home?"

"No, I had to take her without his approval," replied Livia. "Dagmar was crying desperately when I arrived. My heart nearly broke to see her so upset. I just had to bring her home."

"How could you go against the doctor's orders?" Eduard's voice got louder. "Don't you know what could happen to her or to us? What if they send the police after us for defying official orders?"

"Not so loud, Eddek," Livia cautioned. "I am fully aware of the consequences. But, I could not leave the poor child there when she was crying so hard."

"If Dagmar gets worse, no hospital will take her," her husband grumbled.

"Don't try to frighten me," Livia stammered. "I will take good care of my baby. And, I am not afraid of the authorities. At least, I have some backbone, not like you." Before Eduard could reply, the family had arrived at their destination. From the tram, they walked a few steps to their brown, brick apartment block, climbed the stairs to their second-floor flat and unlocked the door. Both parents were out of breath, but that did not stop their argument.

"I will not tolerate insults from my wife," Eduard stated, while Livia laid the baby on the couch and removed her own wet coat and scarf. "I am only concerned for our safety and especially for Dagmar's welfare. Remember what happened to Marlene."

"How dare you throw that up in my face?" Livia's tears started spilling down her cheeks. "What kind of support were you during that dreadful time?" She sank into an armchair. "You pretend to be concerned about the children. Have you forgotten how you abandoned Frank in the middle of *Litzmannstad*?" Livia raised her voice. "Instead of looking after him, you left the little boy on a bench while you went into a bookstore. Then, you forgot all about him. I nearly went frantic when you came home without Frank."

"It was an honest mistake," Eduard defended himself.

"It was totally irresponsible to leave a little child like that," Livia shouted. "I still remember how Frank sobbed when we finally found him." She burst into tears again.

Frank's big, brown eyes clouded over. "Mommy, please don't cry," he pleaded, throwing his arms around her neck. From her blanket cocoon, Dagmar began to whimper. Eduard shrugged his shoulders, turned his back and dived into his study. The slamming door echoed down the hall. Gritting her teeth, Livia stemmed the flow of tears with her dainty lace handkerchief. What was the use of crying over the past? She must get ahold of herself and look after these children.

While Frank glared down the hall, she unwrapped Dagmar and rocked her gently. "Oh, my poor children," she murmured. "What will become of you with a father like that? God, have mercy on all of us, especially now, that the war is escalating."

Gradually, Livia and the children calmed down. After a while, the tired mother placed the baby into her cozy crib. Then, she gave Frank his favorite tin soldiers. As Livia prepared supper, her thoughts wandered. How different life would have been for her if she could have married her first love! I wonder where Sergei Ivanoff is today and what he is doing, thought Livia. If my parents had really known Eduard, they certainly would not have pushed me into this arranged marriage. Will things ever be right between my husband and me? Livia tried to push these disturbing thoughts out of her mind and concentrate on peeling potatoes.

CHAPTER 2

"The German nation must be cleansed of all subversive elements, especially the Jews. To have a true Aryan race, we must find a solution to the Jewish problem," the harsh voice boomed from the radio.

Livia reached across the table and turned the radio off. She dreaded the sound of angry Nazi officials. Why did they hate the Jews so much? Certainly, some underhanded Jews, tried to take advantage of ignorant people, but Livia had very good relationships and business dealings with Jewish people. What kind of a solution to the Jewish problem did the Nazis propose? The tinkling doorbell interrupted her thoughts. She opened the door and found her sister panting on the landing. Lydia waved a newspaper in front of her sister's face. "Please shut the door, Livia," she gasped. "You must see what is in the news today."

Lydia flopped onto a chair and spread out the *"Lodscher Zeitung"* of Feb. 8, 1940, on the kitchen table. "The Chief of Police Announces the Establishment of an Isolated District for Jews," the headline declared. Underneath, was a rough map of the proposed ghetto and a detailed plan for the resettling of Jews from other districts of *Litzmannstadt*. The ghetto was to be established in the most neglected, northern part of the city where many poor Jews already lived.

"How do they plan to pack so many people into such a small area?" exclaimed Livia. "Over one third of our city's population is Jewish,"

"It is the Nazi plan to *"Aryanize"* our nation," answered Lydia. "They intend to get rid of all subversive elements. The Jews will be living only temporarily in the ghetto until the Nazis prepare them for future deportations into other parts of the *Reich."*

"We have lived with the Jews for years without too many problems," Livia twisted her hands together. "How will this order affect the ones we know? It doesn't sound good at all."

"Time will tell," said Lydia. "We must pray for our Jewish friends in the meantime. I picked up that paper on the way over here, but I really came to see Dagmar. How is my favorite niece doing?"

"She has recovered very well. Come and see her. I think she has just woken up from her nap." Livia led her sister into the nursery. The room was painted pink with ruffled white curtains on the window. A teddy bear sat on a stool in the corner beside the white dresser.

Dagmar was sitting up in her crib. She reached out her chubby arms to be picked up. "Oh Dagmar! You look wonderful!" Aunt Lydia jiggled her niece. "Give Auntie a kiss, *Liebling.* I am so glad that you are better now."

With Dagmar in her arms, Lydia went back into the kitchen. Livia was already putting the coffeepot on the stove to make some *Ersatz Kaffee.* The aunt seated her niece in the high chair and gave her a piece of *Zwieback* and a cup of milk.

Late winter sunshine filtered through the lace kitchen curtains onto the embroidered tablecloth. The two sisters sat down to enjoy their afternoon coffee, even if it was only made from ground, roasted grain. This afternoon was pleasant, in spite of the war. They tried to chat about their daily lives. Yet, their conversation always returned to the Jewish question.

"I have an appointment with Dr. Goldberg in two weeks," Livia said. " His office on *Alexanderhof Strasse* will now be within the ghetto quarter. Perhaps, I can get more information about life in the ghetto."

"Yes, maybe there is something we can do for him," Lydia gazed thoughtfully out the window. "He has been very kind to us." She drained the last drop of coffee from her cup.

"Oh, is it four thirty already? I should get home to make *Abendbrodt* for Bruno and me. Please let me know what you find out from Dr. Goldberg." Lydia hugged her sister and kissed Baby Dagmar. Then, she waved good-bye as she hurried out the door.

Two weeks later, Livia went to visit her dentist. From the *Radegast* District where she lived, it was not far by streetcar to Dr. Goldberg's office. She walked the short distance from the tram stop. The tenements along the street were covered with a layer of factory dust that had accumulated over the years. It clung to every crevice, just like the Jewish life in this district.

Livia spotted an old man, wearing a yellow Star of David sewn to his tattered coat. He looked around furtively before darting into a shadowed entrance. The rest of the street seemed to be deserted. She turned the street corner and mounted two steps to the dentist's office. The doorbell had barely rung when the receptionist pulled her inside.

"*Guten Morgen, Frau* Falk," she said. "You are brave to come again to see your Jewish dentist. Don't you know that contact between you and us has now been officially forbidden?"

"Since when?" Livia blinked.

"Ever since the new *Gauleiter* passed this law." The receptionist escorted Livia into the inner office. The middle-aged man with curly black hair and dark eyes was expecting her. Dr. Goldberg greeted his patient warmly and seated her in the chair.

"Before you start to work on my teeth, may I ask how you are doing?" inquired Livia. "We are told that the Jews in the ghetto are being adequately provided for. Don't be afraid to tell me the truth."

"*Frau* Falk, you are one of the few Germans I trust." The dentist lowered his voice. "Conditions in the ghetto are deteriorating every day. More and more Jews from all over are being packed into old, wooden houses. They have no running water or proper sewage system."

"It must be terrible for them!" exclaimed Livia. "Please go on."

"Personal food rations have been cut to a bowl of watery soup each day, a cup of murky brown water that passes for coffee and a loaf of bread to last for five days. I am fortunate to have some food supplies stored, but they will soon run out. How will I feed my family then?" The dentist shook his head sadly. "The Gestapo raided my home last week and took my wife's jewelry and my valuable paintings. Now, I have nothing worth selling. The money we have is only good for use inside the ghetto. We would be executed if we try to leave this place."

"Oh, Dr. Goldberg! This is dreadful news!" Livia gasped, hardly able to keep from weeping.

"That is not all, *Frau* Falk," the dentist continued. "There are daily roundups by the Gestapo. Innocent people are beaten or even hanged. Now, our Elder of the Jews, Rumkowski, has asked us to register for deportation—to work in the *Reich*. Where will all this end?"

"Dr. Goldberg, you must not register for deportation. I have heard bad rumors about those transports," said Livia.

While the dentist prepared his instruments, Livia was lost in thought. Suddenly, she had an idea. "*Herr Doktor*," she blurted out. " I just had an inspiration. My sister and I will bring you a sack of groceries each week. Can you send your oldest son to the north side of the cemetery? It will be a good drop-off point."

"*Frau* Falk, I cannot expect you and your sister to get involved in such a risky scheme," the dentist frowned, shaking his head.

"I have already counted the cost," Livia said firmly, punching her fist on the armrest. "We will come every Thursday afternoon, taking the baby for a long walk along *Gaertner* Street. We can easily hide a sack of food in the baby carriage."

"It is too dangerous, *Frau* Falk!" Dr. Golberg spread his hands and frowned.

Livia continued as though she had not heard. "Your son might pretend to take care of a grave in the cemetery. When we get near the wall, we will start to sing a German song. If your son answers with the call of a crow, we will throw the package over the wall."

"Why do you want to endanger your lives like this for us?" asked Dr. Goldberg.

"We believe that it is our duty to bless God's Chosen People." Livia lifted her chin. "Besides, we do not agree with the Nazi anti-Semitic propaganda."

After the dentist had filled Livia's tooth, she left quickly through the back exit. She walked nonchalantly to the tram stop. The streetcar took her back to her own district.

"Where have you been so long?" Eduard questioned when she entered their apartment.

"I had a dentist appointment with Dr. Goldberg, and he took a little longer than usual," answered Livia.

"It is too risky to be visiting Jewish doctors anymore." Eduard scowled. "Next time, you had better go to a German dentist."

"I know how to be careful," Livia snapped. " Besides, they are in dire need. We should try to help them."

"What do you mean?" Eduard's scowl deepened. "It is against the law to assist Jews. We could be shot if the Gestapo find out."

"You will not have to do anything yourself," Livia spoke soothingly, trying to calm him down. "Please remember that the Bible teaches us to pray for and to bless the children of Israel."

"All right, all right!" shouted Eduard. "I know what the Bible says. "Just don't get yourself into any trouble."

Eduard seemed to dismiss the problem with that statement, but Livia could not get the plight of the Jews out of her mind. With Lydia's help, she would smuggle food to the Goldberg family. She started making plans immediately.

On the following Thursday afternoon, while Frank was at a friend's house, Livia put Dagmar into her pram. She met her sister on the next street corner. Lydia was carrying a bulging bag.

The women hid it under the baby's blanket. What a lovely day for a walk! The last of the winter snow was disappearing under the warming rays of the sun. The two sisters strolled along, laughing and talking. Dagmar's cheeks turned rosy from the fresh air and she smiled with delight at this outing.

After half an hour, they approached the wall around the Jewish cemetery. Livia and Lydia started to sing a German hiking song, "The Wandering Miller". Soon, they heard the cawing of a crow coming from inside the wall. Livia grabbed the bundle hidden under the pram blanket. Lydia kept on singing and watching to make sure the coast was clear. She nudged her sister, who pretended to stumble toward the wall. In a flash, Livia hurled the sack over.

Still singing the hiking song, the two conspirators walked on, away from the ghetto. They breathed sighs of relief when they reached home safely.

Every week, the two sisters repeated a similar charade. They changed their walking route to avoid suspicion. Most Germans avoided the Jewish quarter because they had been warned about the rampant, infectious diseases lurking there. When the women reached the cemetery, they strolled casually along the sidewalk, until they were sure of no observers. They sang patriotic German songs while tossing their package. Any passerby might have thought they were throwing stones to annoy the Jews.

Toward the end of April 1940, new activity bustled around the ghetto. When the two women pushing the baby carriage came closer, they were amazed. Workers were erecting barbed wire fences and extra barricades around the ghetto. A new sign loomed at the entrance.

'RESIDENTIAL DISTRICT OF THE JEWS – TRESSPASSING FORBIDDEN,' the bold black letters proclaimed. A German soldier holding a rifle stood on guard beside the sign.

"We cannot do our food drop today," whispered Livia into Lydia's ear.

"Let us turn around at the corner and walk slowly back," replied Lydia. They pretended that there was nothing wrong, as they wandered away to their own district. The new barriers only presented another challenge to be conquered, in their mission of mercy.

On the next Thursday evening, Livia slipped quietly from her bed after Eduard and the children were fast asleep. She dressed in black clothing and tied a black kerchief over her hair. Then, she tiptoed down the stairs in stocking feet. On the street, she put on her soft-soled walking shoes and waited for Lydia. In a few minutes, a bent old lady, leaning on a cane, limped around the corner. She carried a bundle over her shoulders. Livia almost burst out laughing as she looked at Lydia's face, smudged with streaks of coal. The two sisters linked arms and carefully moved along in the shadows. They had already rehearsed their alibi. "I am taking my sick old mother to the hospital," Livia would say. "She is afraid she will not get fed properly and is carrying her own food parcel."

At night, it took longer than usual to reach the ghetto district. Lydia went ahead a few steps to assess the situation while Livia hid under an overhanging arch. A Gestapo guard with his German shepherd dog was patrolling the wall. Lydia carefully noted the distance of his steps.

Their only chance was to dash across and hurl the package when his back was turned. "I will watch, and when I say ' Go!' you run and toss the sack," Lydia whispered. "We hope that the Goldberg family will get the food somehow." With pounding hearts, the two sisters watched the retreating back of the guard. "Go now!" hissed Lydia.

Livia quickly crept across the street. She was almost there. With all her strength, she threw the sack over the wall. It landed on the other side with a soft thud. Suddenly, loud barking shattered the night.

"Who goes there?" the gruff voice echoed. "Halt, I say!"

Livia was already back, across the street. Shaking violently, she fell into her sister's arms. Lydia drew her sister against a building. They could hear the approaching footsteps of the guard. The dog had quit barking. Was it sniffing out their scent? Where could they hide? They inched along the brick wall.

"God, help us!" they pleaded silently.

All at once, they felt rough wooden planks behind them – a coal cellar door. It yielded to one mighty thrust. They tumbled down into a dark hole. Reaching up, they pushed hard to shut the door. It creaked but held fast. Trembling, the women huddled together in the inky darkness. Blood rushed wildly in their ears. The coal dust tickled Livia's nose. She barely suppressed a sneeze. Both women strained to hear any outside noise. Would the dog find them? Everything was deathly still.

After a long time, the sisters finally dared to move. Carefully, Livia opened the door a crack and peeked out. The streetlight illuminated a bright path toward the ghetto. She saw no sign of the guard or his dog. They must have given up. Cautiously, Livia boosted her sister up through the opening. Lydia glanced along the street. Then, she hoisted her sister up and out. They pulled the coal cellar door shut and slipped away along the dark buildings. Quietly, they crept away from the ghetto. How good it was to reach the safety of their streets!

"We can never do this again," Lydia whispered when they reached home." We were nearly caught tonight."

"Yes, I know," replied Livia. "I am still shaking. We will keep on praying for the Goldberg family, though." Livia hugged her sister before parting. "Good night dear Lydia. I hope you can sleep after this."

In the following weeks, violence against the Jews increased. Livia often wondered what had become of the dentist and his family. She heard of multitudes of Jews being loaded onto cattle cars at the *Radegast* station. Where were they going? What was happening to them? The passing months only brought more arrests.

On a sunny, warm day in August, Livia dressed the children in their best outfits. They planned to go to visit Grandmother Emma, who lived on the south side of the city. Livia carried Dagmar in her arms, while Frank skipped along beside her. At the trolley station, he could hardly contain his excitement. What an adventure – a ride on the tram!

When they boarded the streetcar, they found two empty seats near the middle. Livia sat near a window with Dagmar on her knee, while Frank took the aisle seat. After leaving the *Radegast* District, the streetcar traveled along the *Hohensteine Strasse,* right through the Jewish ghetto. At the entrance, the doors of the trolley were locked. Passengers peered curiously through the windows. Barricades blocked most of the view. Then, the tram passed over a bridge, leaving an unobstructed view of the street below. Livia glanced out through the dirty windowpane. In the distance, she saw a group of Jews, as they pushed an excrement wagon. Two soldiers prodded their backs with rifle butts to make them hurry up. Livia turned her face away in disgust.

"What's wrong Mamma?" asked Frank.

"Nothing, my child," Livia whispered. She tried to divert his attention and hugged Dagmar a little closer.

The tram passed the 'Red House', the ghetto police station. The streetcar lurched and turned into the *Baluter Ring*, where the old market was located.

Some passengers pressed their noses to the windows. Livia looked out to see why. What she saw chilled her to the core. Around the market square were six gallows. From each one, a body dangled on a noose. The corpses swayed like scarecrows in the summer breeze.

"Look at that!" someone yelled. "Serves them right, those dirty Jews! They were probably caught stealing."

Meanwhile, Frank, bursting with curiosity, had climbed up on top of his seat.

"Frank, don't look!" Livia exclaimed. She tried to pull him down, but it was too late.

"Oh Mamma! What happened to those people?" her son gasped.

A young man had overheard the question. "Those are not people. They are sub-humans who pollute our nation. They deserve to die," he spat out.

"But why?" questioned Frank. "What have they done wrong?"

"Sh-sh-sh, Frank," cautioned his mother. "Don't ask any more questions." She turned her son away from the window and shot an angry look at the young man. She could not wait any longer to leave the tram. As soon as it left the ghetto, they would get off.

"In a few minutes we will be getting off, Frank," she said. "Please pull the cord at the next stop."

Livia and the children had to walk ten minutes to Grandmother Emma's house. The young mother gulped fresh air. She wanted to erase those horrible images from her mind.

Somehow, she knew that this was only the beginning of more trouble. She dreaded the return trip through the ghetto. How could she visit her mother and pretend there was nothing wrong?

CHAPTER 3

After the horrors of the ghetto, the familiar gray brick house was a welcome sight. Livia and the children hurried up the stone steps and knocked on the front door. Minutes passed before Grandmother Emma opened it. Her small figure was clad in a flowered housedress, topped with a crisp white apron. A big smile lit up her wrinkled face as she hugged her grandchildren.

"How wonderful to see you!" Grandmother beamed. "Come into the back garden. It is much cooler there." She beckoned them on through the passage to the back door.

Frank dashed out into the yard when he saw a soccer ball lying on the grass. He kicked it hard against the fence. "Be careful with that ball," warned his mother. "Keep it away from the flower beds or the table."

Grandmother Emma led the way to the wrought iron chairs in the shade of the lilac bushes. A matching round table stood nearby. It was covered with a crocheted tablecloth and adorned with a vase of purple asters. Livia fingered the cloth, recognizing the pattern that she had made for her mother. She kept on fussing with the edge as memories flooded her mind. Where had the carefree days of her youth gone?

"How is Eduard doing?" Emma's voice drew Livia back to the present.

"Oh, he is all right, I guess." Livia kept her eyes downcast, as she examined the intricate stitches of the tablecloth.

"What do you mean?" Emma's sharp voice grated on Livia's ears. "You are his wife. You should know."

Livia squirmed in her seat. If it had not been for her mother, she would not be in this love- less marriage now. "Eduard is occupied with the church, preparing sermons and visiting members," replied Livia in a monotone voice. "His health is not good. He coughs a lot and suffers from various aches and pains."

"You must see to it that he gets proper medical care," insisted her mother. "The children need a healthy father who can provide for them."

Livia's head started to throb. She could not tell her mother that Eduard was barely hanging on to his position. Somehow, he had a knack for getting involved in church disputes. If the church split, he would be out of a job. Then, what would they do? Livia had to steer the conversation to a safe topic.

She put Dagmar's feet on the grass. "Run to Frank," she urged. Dagmar toddled off toward her brother. "Look out, your sister is coming," Livia shouted and turned back to her mother. "Mamma, see how well she is walking!"

"Dagmar is growing up so quickly," Emma nodded. "What a blessing God gave you to replace dear little Marlene."

At the mention of her beloved, dead child, Livia quivered. Why did her mother have to bring up another painful topic? Livia wanted to leave the sorrows of the past behind.

"Excuse me, while I play ball with the children," she said to her mother. "We don't often have the chance to play in such a lovely yard." Livia got up from her chair and intercepted the soccer ball.

"Mommy, play with us," shouted Frank. Livia gently rolled the ball toward Dagmar who tried to kick it, just like her big brother. The toddler giggled with delight while Frank impatiently waited for his turn.

Emma watched them play for a few minutes. "I must go into the house and start lunch," she said as she rose from her chair. "Gerda will be home from work soon and she can help me."

Livia was glad that her older, single sister lived with Emma. Since her husband had died, Emma had become withdrawn. Lost in the past, she was often unable to cope with the present. She frequently recalled the injustices, inflicted by the Russians during the last war, as though they had just happened. That was why she had not allowed Livia to become romantically involved with her handsome Russian boyfriend, Sergei. Nowadays, Livia was grateful that Gerda kept a watchful eye on their mother.

Livia and the children were flushed and breathless when Gerda entered the garden. She placed a tray on the table. "Lunch is ready," she called. "Come and wash your hands." Gerda cranked the handle of the creaky old pump, until the water gushed out. Livia and the children happily splashed cold water on their hands and faces. Gerda handed them a towel to dry themselves.

When they were all seated around the table, Emma said the blessing. Then, she passed the open-face sandwiches and dill pickles around. Frank and Dagmar were so thirsty, that they slurped their cold milk. "Not so fast," admonished their grandmother, "You will get a chill."

As a special treat, Gerda brought out the prune plums she had bought at the market. Their lunch was a feast fit for royalty.

Soon, it was time for Livia and the children to say, "*Auf Wiedersehen*" to Grandmother Emma. Gerda accompanied them to the nearest tram stop and waited with them, until the streetcar arrived. The children waved from the window, until they could no longer see their aunt.

On the return ride, the children were tired. Rocked by the movement of the tram, Dagmar soon fell asleep in her mother's arms. Frank leaned against her and dozed off. Their mother also closed her eyes, because she did not want to look at the ghetto again. Instead, images from the past drifted through her mind. She saw herself sitting in her parents'garden again, when her father called her. "Come into the parlor, *Liebling*," he said. "Mamma and I have something important to tell you."

Livia wondered what could be so important. The parlor was reserved for Sunday or for special occasions. Then, Livia, Lydia and Gerda would sing together in harmony, while her father played the harmonium. Usually, Livia looked forward to being in this special room, but today she felt apprehensive. When she entered the parlor, Mamma and Papa were already seated on the high-backed sofa. She gazed expectantly at her parents.

"Livia, you are our youngest child. Now, that you are almost twenty, we thought it time to arrange a suitable marriage for you." Liva's cheeks flushed and then paled. Whom did they have in mind?

"Come, sit down, my child," said her father. Livia's knees felt weak as she gratefully dropped into the armchair. "Mamma and I feel that you need an older man who will give your life stability," her father, Anton, announced. "Our friend, the baker, has a son who is looking for a wife. Eduard Falk has recently graduated from seminary and is applying to become assistant pastor of our church. He would make you a good husband, don't you think?"

Livia's mouth had gone dry. She could hardly believe what she was hearing. "Oh, Papa," she finally croaked. "I can't marry Eduard. I hardly know him. I don't love him."

"Livia, *Liebling*, love will come in time," her mother interrupted. "We want the best for you. Eduard has a chance to be pastor. Your future will be secure and you will be well respected."

By now, Livia was wringing her slender hands. As hard as she tried, she could not prevent the tears from spilling over onto her cheeks. "Mamma and Papa, I want to obey you, but I can not marry Eduard!" she blurted out. When she squeezed her eyes shut, Livia could still see Sergei's handsome face. She had never forgotten the charming Russian soldier who had won her heart when she was only sixteen. If only her parents would have allowed her to marry Sergei.

Livia's heart was pounding as she jumped up. "I will not marry Eduard. You cannot force me to marry someone I don't love." She stomped her foot in frustration. Livia's foot landed forcefully on the toe of the man sitting across from her on the tram.

"Watch what you are doing," he growled at her.

"Oh, I am so sorry," apologized Livia, suddenly brought back to reality. Yet, the vision of the past lingered on. During that fateful interview, Livia might have been able to win her father over, but her mother's tears and endless pleading finally wore her down. In the end, she had agreed to marry Eduard. Now, she was left with only memories of Sergei Ivanoff, and untold regrets. Yet, Livia was determined to do her best to be a good wife. Somehow, she had to make this marriage work.

Livia blinked her eyes and realized that they were almost home. She tried to wake Frank, who yawned and wanted to doze off again. At the *Radegast* stop, she carried sleepy little Dagmar on one arm and dragged her reluctant son behind her. At last, the fresh outside air woke both children. Luckily, they did not have to go far to reach their apartment block.

When the group entered their flat, they found it empty. Eduard was out on church business. Livia settled the children with a few toys and started to prepare supper. What a day this had been!

The warm days of summer soon faded into the crisp days of autumn. It was the beginning of school for Frank. How proudly he posed for a photograph on his first day! He wore his navy blue, sailor suit and carried a *Zuckertuete*—a decorated, cardboard cone filled at the top with candy. The family celebrated the special occasion with a little party after school.

It was not long, though, that Frank came home with Nazi propaganda. "Hitler is the greatest man who ever lived," he proudly declared. "He says that we Germans are the Superior Race. We must squash all others, especially, now, the Russians."

"Frank, please don't repeat everything you hear at school." His mother shook her head. "God wants us to love others."

"But my teacher says that the Russians are *Untermenschen*," Frank replied, wrinkling his forehead and looking puzzled.

"Many Russian people are backward, but they are not sub-humans," Livia tried to explain. "Russian armies have invaded Poland in the past and done horrible things, but I also know of honorable, kind people among the Russians." Of course she was privately thinking of Sergei. Frank seemed to be satisfied with her answer and ran outside to play.

As time went on, Livia had to combat more Nazi propaganda in her young son's mind. Eduard did not concern himself very much except to lose his temper. "Don't say such things around here!" he would yell at Frank.

Signs were everywhere that Hitler wanted to conquer more territory. He had changed his mind about the non-aggression pact that he had signed with Stalin, in 1939. Now, Hitler wanted more *Lebensraum* for Germans in the vast, fertile plains of western Russia. Young German men were conscripted and secretly moved to the eastern border of Poland.

In the spring of 1941, Hitler's new policies began to affect Livia and her family. One day, in May, Gerda stopped by for a short visit. She was almost in tears when Livia opened the door.

Livia stared in astonishment at her usually calm sister and pulled her into the room. "I have bad news!" Gerda blurted out. "My fiancé, Hermann, has been called into the army. He must report to his unit next week. They will probably be sent to the Eastern Front."

"What awful news!" Livia embraced her sister. "Let's hope and pray that he will remain safe."

"I cannot stay long," Gerda said as she wiped her eyes. "Hermann and I want to spend as much time as possible together before he leaves. We plan to go for a long walk in the park today." The sisters hugged once more. Then, Gerda rushed down the stairs.

In a few days, Lydia reported that her husband's firm was being converted for the war effort. Instead of making zippers, they would manufacture vital parts for tanks, Because Lydia's husband, Bruno, was an important foreman, he would not yet face conscription. The *Wehrmacht* was preparing for a renewed push and desperately needed the equipment.

Early on Sunday morning, July 22, 1941, Livia and Eduard woke to bright sunshine. Eduard turned on the radio to hear the usual soothing music. Suddenly, a solemn fanfare rang out, followed by the voice of Joseph Goebbels, Hitler's propaganda minister. He read Hitler's shocking message, justifying the attack on Russia at three o'clock that morning. "What is happening?" questioned Livia as she jumped out of bed and reached for her housecoat.

"Germany is at war with Russia." Eduard clutched the bedcovers to shield himself.

Both of them held their breath as Goebbels read Hitler's final statement. "I have decided, today, to put the destiny of the German nation into the hands of the soldiers again."

"This is madness!" Eduard's voice shook. "A war against Russia means the beginning of the end."

Their quiet Sunday had been turned upside down. Livia and Eduard went through the motions of going to church. They put smiles on their faces and tried to keep their anxiety from the children. After church, groups of agitated people gathered on the street. They discussed the implications of the attack on Russia in subdued tones. The next day, the *Lodscher* Zeitung broadcast the news:

'OPERATION *BARBAROSSA* HAS BEGUN – THE WORLD HOLDS ITS BREATH.'

Livia also held her breath as she scanned daily headlines and listened to the radio. In spite of Nazi optimism, she had her private misgivings. As a child, she had heard about the suffering inflicted by the Russian armies during the last, Great War. Her parents and their children had narrowly escaped from their burning home when the Russian armies attacked their village.

Livia's oldest brother, Erwin, had fought in Russia during winter. He had limped back home after his release from prison camp, in tattered clothes, and with strips of rags bound around his frostbitten feet. He had never fully recovered. "In the Russian winter, you can conquer yourself to death," Erwin had often said.

Operation *Barbarossa* rolled on. According to the reports, the German armies were successfully defeating the Russians before them. If they could win this war before winter, all would be well, but if not . . . The consequences were unthinkable.

By late summer, reports of casualties reached *Litzmannstadt*. Gerda's fiancé was missing in action. New recruits traveled to the Eastern

Front. So far, Eduard's position as a minister and his fragile health had prevented him from being conscripted. Livia tried to carry on her daily routine as always. Yet, in her heart, she knew something ominous lay on the horizon. The German offensive against Russia played on her sensitive nerves.

One night, in late September, Livia awoke screaming. "Hush, Livia." Eduard tried to quiet her. "What is the matter?

Livia's whole body was shaking. "I had a terrible dream," she gasped. "Lydia, Gerda and I were picking mushrooms in the forest when we heard thunder rumbling. We quickly grabbed our pails and started running from the woods," Livia panted. Cold sweat poured from her forehead. "When we reached the road, black clouds billowed around us. Lightening bolts threatened to strike, and a sulfur-like smell engulfed us. It was like hell on earth. We ran as fast as we could. When we finally reached the tram stop, the eastern sky was as black as ink, slashed by ragged lightning." Livia gasped out her nightmare with great effort. Suddenly, she cried, "We must get away from the storm! It will consume us!"

"Be still, Livia." Eduard awkwardly put his arm around his wife. "It was only a dream."

But Livia was already out of bed, searching for her housecoat. Eduard turned on the light.

"Settle down, Livia," he commanded sternly. "You will wake the children. Come back to bed. It was only a dream."

Livia rubbed her eyes. She was fully awake now. "Go back to sleep, Eddek," she murmured and wrapped her housecoat around herself. "I will heat some milk and drink that. Perhaps, I can fall asleep again."

But, Livia did not sleep any more that night. She sat in the soft armchair staring into the darkness. Had God sent this dream to warn her? What did the storm from the East mean? Quietly, Livia prayed for wisdom and protection. After a while she began to relax. Surely, God was in control of her and her family. He would show her what to do in the future.

CHAPTER 4

While the German invasion of Russia continued, Livia's nightmare seemed like a mirage.

Victory was on the side of the Germans. The *Wehrmacht* captured Kiev in the fall of 1941 and drove further east. The Nazi's long-term plan was to completely depopulate Russia by killing the inhabitants, working them to death, or driving them far into Central Asia. Then, they planned to populate the area with German people. Ordinary citizens never knew what was really going on. Only news of German victories broadcast over the airwaves.

In mid-December, Gerda rushed into Livia and Eduard's apartment. She was waving an envelope in the air. "I received a letter from my fiancé, Hermann," she bubbled with excitement. "I thought that I would never hear from him again."

"Please sit down, Gerda," Livia pulled out a kitchen chair for her sister. "I would like to hear what he has to say, if you care to share the information."

Her sister pulled the letter out of the stained envelope and began:

"My dear Gerda,
    I am still alive, here in Russia, writing to you, with ice-cold fingers, from inside my tent.
    My panzer group was lost for a time, cut off by Soviet partisans. We finally managed to rejoin our unit and began attacking. At first, the weather was dry and not too cold,

but then, temperatures fell to −30 degrees. Heavy snowfall hindered our progress. We had to build fires to warm the motors, so that they would start. Soon, we ran short of fuel, because the supply lines have been cut. We have crossed the Moscow Volga Canal and can see the towers of the Kremlin in the distance. Most of us are hungry and shivering in our thin summer uniforms. Now, we are facing tough Soviet divisions dressed in warm winter clothing. They are preparing an offensive. Will we come out alive? Please pray for me.

Your loving Hermann."

When Gerda finished reading she wiped her eyes with her lace handkerchief. Livia also had tears in her eyes. The terrible conditions on the Russian front were unimaginable. "At least, Hermann is still alive," Livia put her arm around Gerda. "Let us pray that he will come back to us." The kitchen clock ticked on, as they bowed their heads in silent prayer.

"I feel a little better now," Gerda rose and grabbed her coat. "I must get back to work, but I just had to let you know."

The conquest of Russia did not proceed as easily as Hitler had anticipated. The Red army proved to be a formidable foe. While German ranks were being decimated, the Soviets drew upon multitudes of reservists in their huge homeland. Hitler's directives to his generals became increasingly irrational. Over the next few years, as *Barbarossa* dragged on and on, men, who had been previously rejected, were drafted into the *Wehrmacht*. Casualties on the Eastern Front mounted daily.

All was not quiet on the home front either. Domestic turmoil troubled Livia and Eduard. When the church split, he had lost his position as assistant pastor. "God will provide," Eduard quoted confidently, but did nothing.

"God helps those who help themselves," Livia shot back. Tired of trying to stretch her meager finances, she knocked on many doors to get another job for Eduard. Finally, she triumphed. Eduard's education qualified him for a position at the Bureau of Statistics. The income helped the family to survive for the time being.

Meanwhile, Frank had developed a negative attitude towards church and refused to attend. "Church is for old people," he insisted. "We only need to believe in the *Fuehrer*." No amount of pleading or threats could change his mind.

The domestic tension culminated in the spring of 1944. In spite of his frail health, Eduard was drafted into the *Wehrmacht*. Now, Livia and the children were forced to manage alone.

Although numerous difficulties had plagued their marriage, Livia worried about Eduard. Was he able to stand the rigors of army life? Eduard had already encountered so many setbacks.

He had inherited his weak constitution from his mother. She had died young, and left behind four children. While his father worked as a baker, Eduard had raised his younger siblings. He developed greater skills at being a nursemaid than becoming a man. His father, Michael, had no sympathy for his oldest son's weaknesses. Using his riding whip, the old man took out his frustrations on Eduard. His son was unfit for physical labor. As a last recourse, Michael sent Eduard to the seminary. Now, Livia's delicate husband was facing the Russians. How could he survive?

Daily, Livia listened for news bulletins on the radio. By now, the United States of America had joined forces with England and Russia against Germany. At the beginning of June 1944, Livia heard this announcement: "From day to day the fighting in Normandy is intensifying . . . the enemy has focused his attention on establishing a foothold on the coast . . . The fighting is approaching a climax." If the Allies did invade France, most of the German forces would be concentrated there, leaving the soldiers on the Russian Front in a precarious position.

"The Russian is finished" Hitler bragged. The reality was much different. The struggle for *Stalingrad* became the turning point. The wicked Russian winter proved to be too much for the *Wehrmacht*. German resistance broke down as their resources were stretched too thin.

Gradually, the Red army forced the Germans back to the curve of the Vistula River near Warsaw. Now, only a few hundred kilometers separated the citizens of *Litzmannstadt* from the Russians.

In the fall of 1944, German officials ordered an evacuation from *Litzmannstadt*. Mothers with small children, elderly and sick people would have to leave. They must report to the leader of their locality for further directions. Livia knew that her city was in grave danger and reported immediately. "You and your children will be transported to the estate of *Hermannsdorf*, the official explained. "It is located in the country, near *Posen*, Take along all your personal belongings except for furniture."

"My elderly mother lives with my sister Gerda in another part of the city," Livia looked at the official with pleading eyes. "My sister is still required to work in the city. Could you arrange for my mother to be evacuated with me?"

"No, that is impossible." The man threw up his hands. "Your mother must be accompanied by a capable person, not a young mother, with her hands full."

Livia was not dismissed so easily. "My sister Lydia lives in my district," she said eagerly. "I am quite certain that she would be willing to accompany my mother."

"Well, if you can convince your sister to go, I will grant official permission," the man said as he stamped Livia's evacuation permit.

A few days later, Lydia obtained an evacuation permit for her mother and herself. She had to temporarily leave her husband who was still working for the war effort. Once settled, she promised to visit Bruno frequently, to check on his welfare. Before leaving *Litzmannstadt*, the three sisters promised to stay together if the time came to flee from the Russians. While Gerda went to work, Livia and Lydia packed. What was important and what could be left behind? They stuffed clothing, linens and personal items into huge suitcases. Their photo albums, full of family memories, must go too. To pack their dishes and cooking utensils, they scrounged up two wooden crates. On and on the packing went. After their last night at home, the women rolled up their feather beds and pillows in old blankets and tied the bundles securely.

In the morning, Livia was looking sadly around the familiar surroundings for the last time, when she heard Dagmar whimper. "Mommy, I want to take my 'Emmie' along," Dagmar reached for her beautiful porcelain doll, lying neglected in the corner.

"Dagmar, *Liebling*," Livia pulled her child away. "You are not allowed to carry any toys on this trip. We are nearly over the limit of the baggage we can take. Kiss your dolly good-bye and leave her here."

Dagmar hugged her doll tightly and after a long kiss, dropped it on the floor. Still sobbing quietly, she turned away and grabbed her mother's hand. With bowed heads, they walked out the door. Frank, wearing a rucksack on his back, was already waiting downstairs. Livia commanded the children to stay together, while she and Lydia brought down the baggage.

'Clip, clop, clip clop', echoed along the cobblestone street. The horses stopped in front of their door. A burly driver jumped down. *"Guten Tag, Frau* Falk." He tipped his cap. "Are these things your possessions?"

"Yes, they belong to my sister and me. On the way to the station, we must pick up my mother with her goods," Livia answered.

"How will I fit everything into my wagon?" The driver scratched his head under his cap.

Then he started to heave bundlers and suitcases into the back. Lydia, Livia and the children crawled onto the bench near the front. Soon, they were on their way. After stopping to get Grandmother Emma and her baggage, the overloaded wagon drove to the railway.

At the station, a mass of people engulfed the new passengers. Livia held tightly to her children's hands while Lydia made sure that their baggage was loaded. Then, they crammed themselves into a packed compartment. It was standing room only. Lydia tried to support her frail mother. How would they be able to breathe in the crush? The train whistle shrilled, smoke billowed from the engine and the train chugged out of the station. The bodies on the train swayed as one. At the next stop a few passengers got off, leaving a little more breathing space. Another stop and then it was time for Livia's group to get off.

Beside the station, a horse-drawn carriage was waiting for them. "I am *Tadeusz Zilinski*, from the estate of *Hermannsdorf*," the Polish driver introduced himself in broken German.

"We speak Polish," Livia answered. "Please help us with our baggage, Tadeusz."

Soon, the coach rumbled along the country road. Strong fall winds had stripped the leaves off the few, widely scattered trees. Stubble-covered fields stretched far into the distance. After a while they passed a small village. "This is where the workers from the estate and from the farms that belong to *Hermannsdorf* live," the Polish driver pointed out. In a few minutes, the coach rolled past magnificent evergreen trees and stopped before an ornate wrought-iron gate. The driver jumped down, opened it, drove the carriage through and closed the gate again. Then, he guided the horses along a circular path, through a lovely park. At last, he stopped before a stone mansion.

The front door of the manor flew open and an elegantly dressed lady, flanked by her maid, stepped out. "Welcome to *Hermannsdorf!*" The lady smiled and threw open her arms. " I am *Frau* Margarethe von Becker and this is Stella, my maid. We have been waiting for you."

Overwhelmed by such a friendly greeting, the coach passengers descended quietly.

"Thank you for your kind welcome." Livia said at last. "We are so grateful to you for taking us in. We hope that we will not be a burden to you."

"Not at all," *Frau* von Becker shook her head. "I am only too happy to help out. And now, you would probably like to stretch your legs and take a short walk to your quarters. Please follow Stella and me." Their hostess and the maid led the evacuees to the carriage house.

The driver was already unloading the baggage. "You will live on the second floor," *Frau* von Becker explained. "My Polish driver and his family live on the lower level. Please make yourselves at home."

The maid ushered Livia and the rest of the group to the upper level. They entered a sitting room with an attached kitchen. A hallway led to two large bedrooms and a bathroom. What wonderful accommodations! "In a few minutes, I will bring over some refreshments," said Stella when she left them. Their driver and another male servant brought up all the belongings into their new home.

Countess von Becker turned out to be not only a good hostess, but also a fount of knowledge. Her husband was a major in the *Wehrmacht* and her son was also an officer. The aristocratic lady had inside information about the war. She knew that the situation for the German army in Russia was extremely precarious. Soviet forces pushed powerfully against the German defense line at the *Vistula* River.

Winter soon broke upon the inhabitants of *Hermannsdorf.* In spite of the upheaval, Livia and Lydia determined to celebrate Christmas for the sake of the children. Their friendly coach driver took Frank and his own son to the evergreen plantation. They cut down a small, symmetrical pine and brought it home. Adults and children alike created ornaments. They made straw stars, and chains from old newspapers. *Frau* von Becker gave them a dozen white candles in metal holders. The decorated Christmas tree was the pride and joy of the evacuees.

On Christmas Eve, everyone gathered around the blazing tree. First, the family shared a special meal. They feasted on bowlfuls of white bread cubes, soaked in warm sweetened milk and sprinkled with poppy seeds. Then, they listened attentively as Lydia read the story of the first Christmas from the Bible. How they longed for the tidings of peace on earth, good will toward men! After the children had received small bags of candy, German Christmas carols rang out in harmony:

"O you joyous, O you blessed, mercy-bringing Christmastime; World was forlorn, Jesus now is born, Rejoice, oh rejoice, all Christian men."

The New Year, 1945, dawned without any celebration at Herrmannsdorf. Early in January, Lydia set out to visit Bruno in *Litzmannstadt.* Among the clothing in her suitcase she carried contraband. The Polish coach driver had illegally slaughtered a pig and given generous portions to the evacuees. In spite of the risk, Lydia was smuggling Bruno's favorite foods—canned pork and sauerkraut.

When she arrived at the train station in *Litzmannstadt*, things were in turmoil. After a recent Russian air attack on the city, all passengers and their luggage were being searched. With shaking knees, Lydia approached the inspector. If the meat was found, she could face arrest and her Polish benefactor might be killed. "What do you have in your suitcase?" the stern official barked. "Quickly, open the lid." When Lydia flipped it up, the pungent aroma of sauerkraut billowed out. The inspector held his nose. "What an awful stink!" he exclaimed and slammed the lid shut. Lydia grabbed her suitcase, breathed a thank you prayer, and raced through the exit.

During the week that she spent in *Litzmannstadt*, Lydia experienced danger first hand. Artillery fire sounded in the distance. Russian bombers circled the city. Suddenly, sirens started wailing. Lydia hurried to the nearest air-raid shelter. She huddled among other frightened people until the all-clear signal came. As the days passed, the attacks became more frequent. Bruno was awaiting orders to dismantle the firm and send the machinery further west. Nothing valuable could be left to the Russians. Each day might be the last one in the city.

Meanwhile, in *Hermannsdorf*, an important telegram arrived from Herr von Becker. Wearing only her housecoat, with her hair completely disheveled, *Frau* Margarethe rushed over to the family under her care. "The Russians have broken through the German defense," she gasped. "They have crossed the frozen Vistula and are coming west."

Livia, who had answered the door, turned white. "What shall we do now?" she cried.

"I will supply you with everything you need," the distraught countess replied, wringing her hands. "We will start immediately to prepare for flight. The Red army will soon overrun our land – killing, raping and plundering."

"But my two sisters are in *Litzmannstadt*. I will not leave without them," answered Livia in a firm tone.

"Then, you had better pray that they get here soon." *Frau* von Becker turned and hurried back to her manor. Livia slowly shut the door. The storm of her prophetic nightmare had been unleashed.

"Dear Lord," she pleaded fervently. "Please bring Lydia and Gerda here safely, soon!"

A frenzy of activity filled the next few days at *Hermannsdorf*. *Frau* von Becker selected two wagons for herself. She had her servants pack her most valuable possessions, and asked the coach driver and another Polish servant to drive. She designated a sturdy covered wagon for Livia and the family. The coach driver chose two sturdy mares to pull it. Then, he loaded eight sacks of feed into the back of the wagon. Food for the journey was an absolute necessity. The servants at the estate slaughtered a pig, cut it into pieces and salted it down. Livia's share was packed into an enamel baby bathtub. Soon, nearly everything was ready.

For such a journey, Livia knew she needed currency. Money was of little value. *Frau* von Becker owned a brewery across the road from the estate. "Take whatever you want," the kind landlady said. Even though Livia had never partaken of alcohol, she realized that it would be the currency she needed. With Frank's help, she lugged two cases of Vodka to their wagon She hid them in the very back, under bundles of bedding.

Even though Livia's hands were occupied, her thoughts were far away. Where were her sisters? Who would drive their wagon? What should she do next?

Litzmannstadt was in utter chaos. The Russians were on the outskirts of the city. Desperate people streamed into the streets, dragging their children on sleds, or pushing dangerously unbalanced handcarts. Bruno had received his orders to go to *Barwald* in *Neumark*. Lydia was packing their remaining things when Gerda stopped by, on her way home from work.

"We must leave right away," Lydia insisted. " You have to come with us. There is no time to go home and get your rucksack."

"But it is ready with all my basic necessities," Gerda couldn't grasp the urgency.

"Put your coat and hat back on. We are leaving now!" Lydia draped the coat over Gerda, grabbed her sister's arm and steered her outside. Streetcars were not running any more. Laden down with suitcases, Lydia, Bruno and Gerda plodded to the train station.

The station was packed with people. They trampled one another, trying to board any train Travelers had no choice but to spend the night dozing on hard wooden benches.

Before dawn, they awoke from their uncomfortable night. Right in front of them, stretchers of wounded soldiers were being loaded onto a train. "Let's go," Bruno nudged the women. He handed his suitcase to Gerda and grabbed the handles of a nearby stretcher.

Lydia and Gerda quickly followed him and the wounded soldier into a train compartment. They squeezed their luggage and themselves into a corner, behind the moaning men.

Slowly, the train pulled away from *Litzmannstadt*. Bruno wanted all of them to go together to his new place of work, but the sisters had made a promise to Livia. When the train stopped at Pleschen, Lydia said a tearful farewell to Bruno. Then, the two sisters left the train and walked ten kilometers to *Hermannsdorf*.

When Livia opened the door for her sisters, she nearly collapsed. She covered her face with her hands and started to weep. "You are here at last," she stammered and hugged them. " I did not want to leave without you."

As tired as they were, Lydia and Gerda had to help. The wagon had to be packed with the rest of the supplies they would need for their perilous journey. The coachman's wife gave them a dozen eggs and a freshly baked loaf of rye bread. While they packed, Livia prayed for someone to drive the wagon. She and her sisters had grown up in the city and were unfamiliar with horses.

Before noon, a truck bearing the insignia of the German *Wehrmacht*, drove up to the coach house. Out hobbled a thin, scruffy looking man. Livia looked out from the top of the wagon in amazement. Quickly, she climbed down. "Eddek!" she shouted. "How did you get here?"

"I spent the last two weeks in the camp infirmary near *Posen*," Eduard answered. " They just released me for ten days of recovery. I could not find you at home in *Litzmannstadt* and was told that you had been evacuated here."

"What an answer to prayer to have you here in time!" Livia hugged him and forgot all past problems. "We need you to drive the wagon. At least you know how to handle the horses."

The emergency was so great that neither Eduard nor the others could afford to rest. The family quickly cooked and ate the pork liver and some bacon, and washed it down with milk that the coachman's wife had provided. Then, they bundled into their warm winter coats. They took one last look around, before leaving *Hermannsdorf.*

At the last minute, Grandmother Emma refused to climb into the wagon. "I don't want to leave," she cried. "Poland is my home. My dear Anton is buried here. Go on without me."

The Polish coachman agreed with her. "She is right," he said. "Don't put an old woman through this in the middle of winter. Your mother is welcome to stay with my family. We will treat her like our own mother and protect her from the Russians."

"You will be lucky if you can protect your own daughters from them," Livia answered in exasperation. "Thank you for the kind offer, Tadeusz, but our mother belongs with us."

Quickly, Livia and Lydia grabbed their reluctant mother by the armpits and hoisted her up into the wagon. Grandma Emma was still sniffling when she collapsed onto the feather beds in the back. The two sisters jumped up onto their wooden seats. Eduard took the reins, clicked to the horses and they drove off into the unknown.

CHAPTER 5

Wooden wheels creaked through the crisp winter cold. The horses snorted out clouds of freezing breath. On the covered wagon, the group of refugees huddled together as they bounced along the frozen road. In the back, Gerda put her arm around Grandmother Emma and murmured soft words of comfort to her. Lydia, on the side bench, hugged Dagmar and Frank. Livia occupied the front seat beside the driver, Eduard. He guided the horses towards the south—west. One main wish coursed through Livia's mind—escape from the Russian hordes behind them. Their only hope was to reach Silesia where her brother Ehrenfried and his wife Anna lived.

The lack of sleep and tension stretched every nerve to the breaking point. They had driven only a few kilometers when Livia felt like she was suffocating under the heavy canvas canopy. She reached into the box of cutlery and grabbed a sharp knife. "I must get some fresh air!" she cried and slashed the canvas above her head. Shaking violently, she gulped quick breaths of cold air.

"Look what you have done," scolded Eduard. "Now, the snow can get in through that hole."

Livia only stared vacantly into the darkening afternoon of January 20th, 1945. She fought to gain control of the drumming in her ears. "Oh, God, help us all," she gasped. "Help us to get away from our enemies."

Full of questions, Dagmar's eyes searched her aunt's face. "Where are we going, Auntie?" she asked.

"*Liebling*, I really don't know," Lydia answered and cuddled the child a little closer.

"Wherever it is, we know that the Lord is with us. He will take care of us. So, please be a good girl."

"I hope we will find a proper place to spend the night," interjected Frank. "My bottom is already sore from sitting on this hard bench."

His hopes were in vain, because his father did not dare to stop. Artillery fire lit up the dark sky and cannons boomed in the distance. The Soviets were not far behind. They drove on through the night without meeting any other refugees. Before dawn, Eduard stopped the wagon briefly, so that everyone could relieve themselves behind trees and bushes.

All through the next day, the hard-working horses pulled the heavy wagon. The passengers did not dare to stop anywhere, more than a few minutes. How thankful they were for the loaf of bread and the eggs that the coachman's wife had sent along! Lydia held the bread under her coat, next to her body, until it had thawed enough to break off a few chunks. Then, each person chewed the portion very slowly. For each of the children, she broke a raw egg into a cup and beat it with a fork until the egg liquefied. She encouraged Frank and Dagmar to swallow the contents

"Aw, yuck!" exclaimed Frank, made a face, but gulped it down.

Dagmar wanted nothing to do with this unfamiliar drink. She clamped her lips shut when her aunt handed her the cup. In desperation, Lydia held the child's nose until her mouth opened.

"Now, swallow this", she coaxed, as she tipped the cup over Dagmar's lips. The little girl gagged at the first mouthful. After more coaxing, she swallowed a few more gulps.

At nightfall, the refugee family reached an empty house. The occupants had fled, leaving their livestock behind. Livia and the others were dreadfully tired and longed to stretch out for a rest. When they entered the kitchen, a group of German soldiers were cooking a pig, which they had taken from the barn. Although the food smelled delicious, the newcomers only wanted to sleep. Still wearing their coats, they dropped onto bare mattresses in a cold bedroom. Eduard was still in the barn, looking after the horses, when he heard a motorcycle roaring into the yard. He stepped outside to see who had come.

"What are you doing here?" a German soldier yelled at him. "Don't you know that the Russians are nearby? You must get away immediately!" With that, the soldier turned his motorcycle around and raced away into the night.

Eduard hurried back into the house to wake the others. "Get up!" he cried as he entered the bedroom. "We must leave at once. The Russians are close by. Hurry up, and get back on the wagon!"

The weary ones groaned, and started to move very slowly. Livia picked up sleepy little Dagmar, while Lydia steered Frank, as he tottered toward the door. Gerda had a difficult time trying to rouse her mother. Finally, she scooped up the old woman, draped her over her back and carried her out to the wagon. Meanwhile, Eduard had been fumbling around in the dark to hitch up the horses. At last, the family was back on the wagon, ready to go.

Once again, the horses' hooves clip—clopped along the frozen gravel. All hope of sleep left Livia and Eduard. Would they ever find a safe place to rest? During the night, a military vehicle passed by them and pulled up in front. A soldier leaned out. "Where are you going?" he asked in fluent German. "Why are you fleeing? Have you seen any other military going past?"

"We are traveling west," she replied, cautiously, poking Eduard in the ribs to keep him quiet. "We are on our way to visit my brother. No, we did not see any German military on this road."

"A safe journey to you, then" the man replied. The car roared away, down the road ahead of them. Livia was relieved when he left. Could he and the other men in the car have been spies for the Russians? Luckily, the rest of that night's journey was uneventful.

By morning, they joined a group of wagons heading west. Suddenly, they heard a panzer unit approaching. The German military had the right of way on all the roads. Eduard tried to steer the horses off the road, but the tanks were already rolling down the middle. Their tracks brushed against the wagon wheels and got caught. The wagon lurched crazily. "Have mercy on us, O God!" Livia yelled. Eduard strained to keep the horses steady. When it seemed that they would all perish, an unseen hand loosened the wagon wheels from the tracks. They were safe! Although the passengers were still in shock, the wagon kept on rolling. As the darkness descended, they took a side road into a forest and stopped for a while. How desperately they needed a proper night's rest!

Eduard's eyes were bloodshot from lack of sleep. He could no longer see what was ahead. "Please let me sleep for a few hours," he pleaded.

"You can close your eyes for half an hour, but no longer," Livia grabbed his arm and looked sternly into his face. "The Russians are still far too close. We must not fall into their clutches. I can still hear cannon fire in the distance."

"I cannot keep on driving," Eduard groaned. "Have pity on me."

"I will be your eyes," Livia said firmly. "My children will not fall into enemy hands."

After half an hour, the wagon started out again. Eduard held the horses' reins, while Livia peered out ahead and gave directions. "Drive straight ahead. Turn right. Turn left," she ordered. Through sheer force of will, they traveled on.

On the fourth day of their flight, they arrived at a small Polish village. Perhaps, they could stay here for a while? While Eduard and Frank fed and watered the horses, Livia entered a nearby house. "*Prosze Pani*, may I boil some water?" she addressed the woman in Polish. "My family and I would be grateful if we could rest here for a few hours."

The round-faced peasant smiled at Livia. "Welcome to my home," she replied. "You may use my stove and your people can rest in my front room."

"Thank you, and God bless you," Livia said and ran outside to call the others. How thankful they were to stretch out! A hot meal satisfied their hunger. Afterwards, they each found a place to rest. Grandmother Emma stretched out on the sofa. Eduard and Livia lay back in soft armchairs. The aunts and the children curled up on a rug in the middle of the floor. Sleep at last!

Only minutes seemed to have passed, when loud pounding shook the front door of the house. Several German military police stormed into the kitchen. "Where are you hiding the refugees?" they shouted to the Polish woman. With a frightened look, she pointed to the front room. The leader barged in upon the sleeping family. "Get up at once!" he barked. "The Russians are close behind. You must get on your wagon and hurry away while there is still time."

Groaning and rubbing their eyes, Livia and Lydia rose first. They shook Eduard awake and carried the sleeping children out to the wagon. With much effort, Gerda managed to carry Grandmother outside. After the tired horses were hitched up again, the wagon rolled out of the village. Would this endless flight ever end?

Violent artillery fire shook the ground. Nearby, German and Russian armies were in close combat. The German military needed to use the road. All other vehicles were forced off.

Eduard yanked on the reins and the horses veered onto the frozen fields. The wagon clattered violently across the ruts. Gerda held onto her mother's head to prevent it from flying back and forth. They all bounced wildly on the wooden seats until their teeth rattled. Finally, they reached another road. What a relief it was to ride smoothly!

"I cannot drive anymore," moaned Eduard and dropped the reins. Artillery fire exploded all around. Closer and closer, lumbered monstrous Russian army tanks. Livia gasped as other wagons were mercilessly crushed beneath their treads.

"You will not let the Russians destroy us, now," yelled Livia. She grabbed the reins and whipped first Eduard, and then, the horses. "Get into the back of the wagon and sleep there with Grandmother," she shouted. The horses bolted away onto a side road. Livia, who had never controlled them before, guided the animals for the rest of that day. She gritted her teeth to keep going in spite of the illness that tore at her bowels.

A huge moon lit up the sky when they reached a large, abandoned house. Eduard and Frank un-hitched the horses and sheltered them inside the barns. Those hard-working animals certainly deserved a rest. Meanwhile, the rest of the family entered the house.

They found enough wood to make a fire in the kitchen stove. Using their own supplies of frozen pork, they soon cooked a delicious meal. Soon afterwards, everyone was fast asleep on the bare mattresses in the bedroom.

After a good night's rest, the travelers felt better. When they had eaten some bread, they left for another day on the road. Livia hunted around in her baggage to find a strong needle and thick thread. While Eduard drove, she repaired the gash in the canvas covering. They needed the protection against the cold wind and the snow. She found it hard to sew while standing up on the jiggling wagon. Yet, she had to repair the hole she had made in the first place.

Another long trek took the travelers a little farther away from danger. During the day, they traveled past snow-covered fields and abandoned farms. That evening they arrived at a village flooded with refugees. They found accommodation in a large house. Because strange, unsavory-looking characters milled around on the yard, Lydia decided to stay on the wagon and guard it overnight. She wrapped her overcoat tightly around herself and then pulled another featherbed over top to cover her body. At least she would stay warm while on guard duty.

Inside the house, a group of German soldiers sat around the kitchen table. They drank till late into the night. Just as she was falling asleep in the bedroom, Livia heard a thump. One of the drunken soldiers had fallen off his chair. At least, the refugees could doze off now, because none of those fellows would bother them.

When Livia went into the kitchen early next morning, the men were still sleeping off their binge. While she made breakfast for her family, she saw boxes of liquor along one wall. At the table, an officer with his head on the table, held a half-empty bottle of vodka.

Liva had a sudden idea. "That bottle might come in handy on the rest of our journey," she whispered to herself. Softly, she crept over to the table and slowly wriggled the bottle out of the sleeper's hands. Another refugee woman was watching the process.

"Why are you going to so much trouble when full bottles are sitting in these boxes?" She pointed to the crates. "These soldiers stole them anyway. So you might as well take another one." Livia glanced cautiously around the room and then, quickly took another bottle of vodka. She did not add them to the other bottles in the wagon, but she kept the new bottles under her seat, at the front.

Later on, during the extremely cold weather, the liquor became a lifesaver. With the Russians in close pursuit, the refugees could not afford to stop for meals. Instead, each adult took one sip of vodka, while Eduard took two. The children received a drop of liquor in their raw egg mixture. The fiery liquid briefly warmed their insides.

During the sixth day, their wagon joined another long trek on the road. They neared a park- like area just as it was getting dark. Suddenly, a man jumped in front of their wagon and grabbed the horses' reins. He pulled them off the road and onto the drive leading into the park. "Stop it! What are you doing?" yelled Eduard, to no avail.

When they had gone deep into the park, the man stopped and peered into the wagon. "You don't look like the people I was supposed to get," he exclaimed. "Well, it is too dark to go back. You might as well spend the night here." With that, he ran off, down the drive toward the manor house. Livia, Eduard and the family did not dare to knock on the door. They took small sips of vodka and spent the night on the cold wagon.

In the morning their frustration turned into thankfulness. Sleet had fallen during the night, turning the road into a sheet of ice. The wagons that had kept on going met a terrible fate. In the dark, horses had lost their footing and skidded down steep embankments. Broken wagon wheels, scattered belongings, injured and dead people and animals littered the ditches.

Eduard and Livia could not stop to help anyone, for their own lives were in danger. In the daylight, Eduard kept the horses to the center of the road. Livia prayed that their hooves would not slip. As soon as possible, the wagon veered off to a safer side road.

Later that day, the refugees entered an evergreen forest. Thick, fluffy snowflakes tumbled from the sky and covered the trees in mantles of white. The absolute stillness of these pristine woods formed a stark contrast to the terror all around. In the middle of this beautiful place, they found a little house. A young, German couple welcomed them with open arms. The husband was a civil servant in the nearby city. His wife was about eight months pregnant.

"Why are you not getting ready to flee?" asked Livia.

"Oh, there is still time," the young man replied. "I am waiting for an official order to leave."

"And I am waiting for the fur coat that I ordered for our journey," added his wife.

"I hope that your coat comes before the Russians do," said Livia, shaking her head at such complacency.

The next morning, everyone waved good-bye to the friendly couple. As they drove on, they wondered what would happen to these kind people. Would they still escape from the Russians?

That day, the travelers continued on in their gypsy-like existence. On and on, they journeyed. They joined another trek of refugees, but as soon as possible, veered away on side roads. At night, they bedded down on straw, on the floor of a former youth hostel. They were grateful for any place to rest their weary bodies. German soldiers, retreating from the Soviets, occupied another section of the house. When they saw Livia's 'currency', the soldiers gladly shared food with the newcomers.

As the travelers began their journey the next day, enemy bombers circled low overhead. Loud machine gun fire shook their wagon. Some bullets strafed the wagon ahead of them.

They must get off this road, quickly. Eduard steered their wagon onto a country road, away from the other wagons. The bombers continued to harass the main trek, but their wagon was safe.

After keeping to the side roads, the fleeing family reached the crossing of the *Oder* River, near *Glogau*. As they approached the bridge, Livia saw that the supports had been laced with explosives. Soldiers with detonators in their hands stood by. "Pray that we make it across this bridge safely," she yelled into the back of the wagon. Her heart pounded violently as their wagon rolled across the bridge. "Thank God! We are safe," she exclaimed when they reached the other side. They were only a short distance away, when a loud blast shook the earth. A cloud of debris obscured the sun. The bridge was gone.

Through the bitter cold, the family trekked on and on. Ten days after they had left *Hermannsdorf*, Livia, Eduard and the family arrived at their destination. *Penzig* was a small town near the city of *Goerlitz*, in Silesia. Their brother, Ehrenfried, and his wife lived here. Their sister-in-law, Anna, welcomed them. "We have been waiting for you since your letter arrived." She stammered out between tears. "We were afraid something terrible had happened to you. Now, you can have the rooms we have prepared. Ehrenfried is still at work in Goerlitz. How happy he will be to see you!"

The road-weary "gypsies" could hardly believe what they heard. Was it possible that they could stay here? To sleep in comfortable beds and eat regular meals would truly be a luxury. This place would be their new home.

CHAPTER 6

What a welcome the weary travelers received at this humble home! When Ehrenfried arrived from work in the evening, he hugged each family member. "Thank God, that you made it here safely!" he exclaimed. He and Anna went out of their way to make their relatives comfortable. They set up bunk beds in the bedrooms. Now, the visitors could sleep peacefully at night.

The next morning, Eduard said good-bye to the rest of the family. His 'days of rest' were over and he had to report back to the military. "Take care of yourself and stay safe," Livia wished him when they parted. Would Eduard survive another period of service in the *Wehrmacht*?

Plenty of work occupied minds and hands during the next few days. The pork that they had brought from *Hermannsdorf* had to be processed. Anna supplied the necessary jars for canning the meat. The fat was rendered into creamy, white lard. Then, the women fried some lard with onions to make a spread for their dark, rye bread. It tasted wonderful with a cup of hot cocoa. While the women were cooking, Ehrenfried took the horses to board at a nearby farm. Later, he pushed the wagon into an empty corner of his yard.

Every day, all ears were tuned to the radio for news of the war. In spite of political optimism, the tide had turned against the Germans. One day, the announcer listed the areas now occupied by the Soviets. Among these, was Barwald, Neumark. Lydia's heart skipped a beat.

"My husband is now in Soviet territory. What will happen to him?" she moaned. No one knew the answer.

Livia put her arm around her weeping sister. "He is in God's care," she whispered. "Let us pray that he will come out of this alive." Soon, the air was filled with petitions for God's protection for their men.

After one week, Livia discovered that Penzig was not the end of their flight. She had not been feeling well that morning, when she answered the doorbell. A young fellow thrust an envelope into her hands. She tore it open to find a letter from the mayor's office. "All refugees owning horses and wagons are ordered to leave Penzig in three days," the message stated. Livia began to shake. How could they leave without someone to drive their wagon?

Suddenly, the room spun around her. With a loud thump, Livia collapsed on the floor.

Lydia, who had been working in the kitchen, rushed over to help her sister. Livia's face was white, but her skin felt hot. The notice had fluttered out of her hand. "Oh no!" Lydia cried.

"Not this! Not now!" She took deep breaths to calm herself. First, she must care for her sister. She slowly dragged Livia onto the couch. Then, she ran back into the kitchen and returned with a cold wet cloth. When Lydia placed it on her sister's forehead, the patient's eyes flew open.

"Where am I?" Livia mumbled thickly.

"You are resting on the couch." Lydia stroked Livia's dark hair. "Please, lie still. You are not well."

Livia tried to get up but fell back. "I feel awful," she croaked.

"Take it easy," Lydia said firmly. "I will bring you a glass of water." After Livia had gulped down the water, her eyes closed again. Lydia covered her sister with a blanket.

She could do no more. No doctor or medicine was available. "Dear Lord, please heal Livia," she prayed as she went back to her work.

When Gerda returned from an errand in town, the sisters carried Livia into the bedroom. They took turns bathing her with cool water. While Livia was burning up with fever, her sisters also needed to care for the children and their elderly mother. The order to leave Penzig weighed heavily on their minds. Where could they turn for help?

That afternoon, Lydia dressed in her best clothes and went to see the mayor. She paced the waiting room floor for almost an hour before being admitted into his office. The heavy-set man, overflowing out of his chair, glared at the newcomer.

"Your Honor," Lydia bowed to the important man as she placed their identification papers on his desk. "We are a family of refugees who arrived here one week ago. My brother-in-law, who was driving our wagon, has been recalled to the army. No one else knows how to handle the horses. If we must leave, please provide us with a driver for our wagon."

"I sincerely regret that I am unable to help you." The mayor shook his head as he scrutinized the papers before him. Then, he looked up into Lydia's tear-filled eyes. Quickly, he scribbled a note on an official piece of paper. "Take this to the prison camp on the east side of the city," he added. "I have asked the commandant to supply you with a French prisoner to be your driver."

"Thank you very much, sir." Lydia bowed again and rushed out of the room, clutching the paper. After walking for half an hour, she arrived at the gate of the camp. She showed the paper to the guard and was immediately admitted. The guard pointed her to the big hut in the center of the camp. Lydia knocked on the door.

"Come in," a deep voice boomed out. She entered a small room. Behind a desk, littered with paper, sat the balding military commander. "How can I help you?" he asked politely. Lydia placed the mayor's letter into his hands and stood, praying quietly. The commandant glanced over the note. "My dear lady," he apologized. "I cannot give you a driver until we have received the order to liquidate this camp. Please, return every morning and evening to find out when we will be leaving. I regret that I am unable to give you a more definite answer. *Auf Wiedersehen!*" With that he waved Lydia out. Tired and discouraged, Lydia returned home.

In order to get a driver, Lydia had no choice but to walk to the camp and back, twice a day. To aid her request, she took along a bottle of Livia's 'currency' to give to the commandant.

Meanwhile, Livia was still delirious with fever. Worries increased as distant artillery fire came closer. They had to get away before the Russians arrived.

Next morning, the town was in turmoil. When Gerda went to get the milk ration for the children, she heard women crying as she entered the store. "The Russians are coming!" they sobbed. "The French prison camp has been liquidated. The German soldiers who guarded them have all disappeared."

Running as fast as she could with the milk, Gerda brought home the bad news. Lydia grabbed her coat and hurried to the east side of town, but the prison camp was empty. She walked back slowly, tears spilling over her cheeks. "We are lost without a driver," she cried out to a neighbor who was loading a hand wagon with his possessions.

"Wait a minute," the man shouted back to her. "I want to get to my mother's place, sixty kilometers west of here. If you allow me to hook my handcart onto your big wagon, I will drive for you."

For a moment, Lydia stood in stunned silence. Then, the thunder of approaching cannon fire shook her back to reality. "Oh, thank you, sir," she blurted out. "You may hook your cart on right now. When you have finished, please get our horses from Farmer Schultz. We will be ready to leave by the time you return."

"We have a driver! God has heard our prayers!" Lydia shouted as she ran into the house.

"Hurry up! We must pack everything right away." A flurry of activity filled every room. Bedding, clothing and food had to be packed and loaded onto the wagon. How thankful the sisters were that Livia was feeling a little better! At least, she could keep an eye on the children and Grandmother Emma.

During all the commotion, Lydia and Gerda pleaded with Anna. "Pack your basic necessities and come with us." Lydia grabbed Anna's arm. "You can leave a note for Ehrenfried telling him where you have gone."

"I will not leave my home!" Anna pulled away from Lydia. "If I have to be forced out of my home, I would rather die. I must stay here for Ehrenfried's sake also."

"Anna, please be reasonable." Lydia tried again. "When the Russians come, you will not have time to escape."

"No!" Anna stamped her foot. "You go on your way. I cannot leave all my possessions like this."

Tired of arguing, Lydia and Gerda finished packing the wagon. Grandmother Emma slumped on the couch, staring vacantly into space. Frank scurried about, stuffing a few things into his rucksack. Dagmar gazed around with huge eyes. "Where are we going now?" the child asked. No one could answer the question they were all asking.

Finally, Livia gathered her strength and heated some soup. "Come and have a little bit of nourishment." She coaxed the children to the table.

They slurped down a bowlful and munched on a slice of bread. The adults did not sit down, but gulped their food standing up.

Then, they struggled into their winter coats and hats. With quick hugs and tears, they parted from Anna. From the warm house, they stepped out into the icy air. Grandmother Emma was the last one to leave. Before reaching the wagon, she stiffened up and refused to move. "Leave me. I am too weak and old for all this roaming around."

"You are coming with us," Livia said firmly. "We have brought you this far. We are not going to leave you here for the Russian wolves."

Lydia and Gerda put their arms around their fragile mother. With one heave they lifted her upon their shoulders and carried her into the wagon. The old woman moaned as she flopped onto the familiar featherbeds in the back.

Quickly, the others scrambled up the little side ladder, into the wagon. The friendly neighbor jumped up into the driver's seat. Livia sat beside him, just like she had with Eduard. With a flick of the whip and a click of the tongue, the horses began to trot down the street, pulling the heavy load behind them. How thankful the travelers were that the Russians were still behind them!

CHAPTER 7

A strange hush hovered over the land, as the covered wagon and its attachment rolled out of Penzig. The barrage of artillery fire had ceased. Quiet, snow-covered fields stretched into the horizon. Were the occupants of the wagon just taking a leisurely drive along the countryside? The illusion was shattered only a few kilometers down the road.

Suddenly, a lantern flashed in front of the driver. A man's voice shouted, "Halt!"

"Whoa!" The driver strained hard to pull back the reins. With a skid, the horses stopped in front of the military policeman.

"Where are you going?" demanded the man in uniform. "Why are you not with the *Wehrmacht*?"

"I am only driving for these people because I was injured earlier in the war, and have been declared unfit to serve." The driver's voice shook. "We are on our way to my mother's home, about sixty kilometers west."

"How many people are in this wagon?" The policeman shone his flashlight into the interior.

"We have four women and two children, beside myself," the driver stammered.

"Are there any men hiding under all that baggage in the back?" the officer demanded in a stern tone. Obviously, he was looking for deserters from the army.

"No, sir," Livia spoke up. She was clenching her shaking hands. "Our men are away, fighting bravely against the enemy."

The officer shone his light into every face. "You may proceed," he said at last and waved them on. With a loud sigh, Livia let out the breath she had been holding. What a close call!

The remaining distance sped by uneventfully. The wagon turned off the main road into a small village. The horses strained uphill with their heavy load. At the top, stood a cluster of brick houses. "That is my mother's place." The driver smiled as he pointed to the tiny house in the middle. In a few minutes, he stopped the horses at the front door.

The lace curtain on the big window shifted and a face peered out. A few minutes later, a white-haired lady opened the door. When she saw who was descending from the wagon, she hurried outside. "Werner, my son!" she exclaimed, pulling him into a tight embrace.

"*Mutter*, you will catch cold out here." Werner kissed her cheek and pulled her into the house. " I have brought guests with me."

Immediately, the old woman poked her head out again. "Pardon me for being rude." She squinted her eyes, peering up into the wagon. "Please come down and enter my little home." She beckoned with her hand. The frozen travelers gladly obeyed and climbed down from the wagon. Soon, they huddled around the warm stove in the parlor. Their hostess wanted to know all about their journey and plied them with many questions. What a treat it was to have company! At last, she realized that her guests were hungry and tired. She scurried around in the kitchen, preparing a hot meal. After they had eaten, the visitors' eyes started drooping.

Werner led them to a spare bedroom. Soon, the adults were sleeping two to a bed. The children rested on feather beds spread over the rug in the middle of the floor. Even though the family would have gladly stayed, they did not know how close the Russian armies were.

Now that Werner had arrived at his destination, they needed another driver. Someone had to find a suitable person. Livia was still weak from her illness, but Lydia took up the challenge. After breakfast, the next day, she dressed warmly and walked down the hill to the main road.

Groups of retreating German soldiers and prisoners marched slowly past. Lydia hoped to see the familiar field marshal from Penzig with his group of French prisoners.

The cold morning passed very slowly. Lydia stamped her feet and rubbed her hands to keep warm. At noon, Lydia stumbled up the hill. "I feel chilled to the bone," she stammered between chattering teeth, when she entered the warm house. After gulping down a bowlful of hot soup, Lydia was determined to go back. She would not miss any opportunity to get help.

The afternoon dragged on as Lydia watched the road. She was numb from the cold, and ready to give up, when she saw a small group of men approaching. Before she could reach them, they turned off the road and marched up the hill. Lydia scrambled uphill behind them. The officer led the men into a large, empty house near Werner's mother's place. Lydia knew that the men would need food and a good rest before she dared to make her request.

"I think we will be lucky!" Lydia burst into the kitchen with a smile on her face. She pointed out the window. "An officer and twelve prisoners are quartered in the big house over there. We will ask them for help tomorrow."

Next morning, Livia felt strong enough to accompany her sister. Under her arm, she carried a bottle of her 'currency.' The two women looked pleadingly at the uniformed man who answered the door. "*Sehr geehrter Herr,*" Livia said politely. "We belong to a family of refugees from Poland. We desperately need a driver for our wagon. My husband, who was driving, is back in the army, and the man who brought us here can go no farther. Please, sir, can you give us one of your men to be our driver?" Livia pushed the bottle into his hands.

"*Meine lieben Damen.*" The officer made a tiny bow. "I would really like to help you, but first, you must meet certain requirements."

"We will do whatever you ask," Livia and Lydia exclaimed in unison.

"If I provide one of the prisoners to be your driver, you will be under my command," the officer replied. "You must travel with my troupe wherever we go and obey all orders."

"We gladly accept your kind offer," Livia said joyfully. Lydia nodded her head in agreement. "Please, inform us when you plan to leave again."

"Be ready to go at seven tomorrow morning," the officer ordered. "I will have my man hitch up your horses to your wagon."

"*Vielen Dank!*" Livia smiled and bowed lightly. The sisters ran back to tell the others the good news.

When they started out the next morning, the refugee family had no destination. Their only aim was to escape from the Russians. Their wagon traveled behind the officer and his prisoners. The troupe took a northwesterly direction toward a pre-arranged rendezvous.

The refugees rode through the winter landscape as though in a dream. Never again could they return to the homes they had left far behind. At every stop, they heard about the brutality of the Russians, who were taking revenge on the fleeing Germans.

Livia was lost in deep thought. Somehow, she could not imagine that the cultured Sergei she had known could act like those savages. She wondered where he was fighting right now. Livia shook herself to blot out the memories.

In the late afternoon, the leading officer signaled a stop. The prisoners started to dig around in a handcart they had been pulling. Out came a portable stove and sacks of provisions. The prisoners scrounged around in the ditch for dry sticks of wood. Before long, they had a fire blazing. Then, they scooped up clean snow into a huge pot and set it on the stove. The prisoners started skinning two plump wild rabbits. By this time, the family had climbed down and looked on in amazement. Where and when had the men snared those animals? When the water started to boil, the cooks dropped in pieces of meat, some chopped onions and small potatoes in their skins. They added a dash of salt from a small tin and covered the pot. Soon, a tantalizing aroma emerged from the simmering stew.

While the men were busy, the women and children hid discreetly behind bushes to relieve themselves. Attending to the call of nature was always a problem along the way. They kept a covered chamber pot on the wagon for emergencies.

When the rabbit stew was ready, the officer invited everyone to partake. One of the prisoners drew out a round loaf of dark, rye bread from their sack. The cook served each.

"I believe this is the best meal I have eaten in a long time," Livia declared. "Thank you for this road-side feast." After washing the dishes in heated snow water, the men packed the stove, and other utensils into their handcart. With full stomachs, they walked a little slower, until night fell.

That night a barn offered sufficient accommodation. Livia, her mother, sisters and the children bedded down on the hay, in one corner. The officer and his men slept in the other corner. None of the women felt threatened by their companions, because their commander kept a tight rein on his men.

Day after day, the aimless existence continued, as the wagon rolled amid the prisoners. The captain allowed no misdemeanors among the captives. Yet, when he was not looking, the kind Frenchmen offered little pieces of chocolate from their own Red Cross parcels to the children. Frank was delighted, but Dagmar scrunched up her lips and refused to taste the unfamiliar brown stuff. "Try it, Dagmar," urged Frank. " It tastes very good." Finally, his little sister licked a piece of chocolate. Her face lit up with pleasure. After that, she couldn't get enough.

After several days of traveling, the officer and his troupe reached their meeting point, in a small town. He joined his captain who had more prisoners under his command.

Carrying the usual currency, Livia and Lydia went to see the new leader. "Please, sir," they pleaded. "Allow us to travel with you. We are dependent on the man who has been driving our wagon."

"If you promise to obey my commands, you may travel with our company," the captain replied, and took the bottle they offered.

"We will gladly do so." The women bowed to the captain. "*Vielen Dank, Mein Herr.*"

Now, a long train wound its way along the road. In front of the column, limped the captain and his sergeant. The captain had been wounded earlier in the war and the sergeant had lost several toes to frostbite, when he fought on the Eastern Front. Behind them, came the wagon, followed by seventy-two prisoners. The non-commissioned officer, who had led the prisoners earlier, made up the rear. Even though the leading men suffered greatly from their injuries, they rarely accepted an invitation to ride on the wagon.

Under the captain's leadership, the others quickly learned a life-saving routine. When Russian bombers roared overhead, the men quickly dived into the ditches beside the road. The wagon's occupants clambered down as fast as possible. They threw themselves, face-down, into the ditches. "The reflection from your faces is a target for the enemy," the captain had shouted. When it was safe, they climbed back onto the wagon and continued on their way. They never knew when the process would have to be repeated. The captain carefully avoided large cities. Instead, he sought shelter for the night in small villages.

One night, the company arrived at a farm in Saxony. While the officers and prisoners settled down in the barn, the family sought shelter in the house. A big, unfriendly woman answered the knock on the door. "May we have shelter here for the night," Livia asked gently. "We have traveled far and are very hungry and tired."

"I suppose I have no choice but to let you in." The woman scowled at the intruders. "You can use my stove, but don't leave a mess," she added, pointing toward the kitchen. While the others settled down on wooden benches beside a large table, Lydia went back to the wagon to get a jar of canned pork.

Livia screwed up her courage once more. "Would you be so kind as to give us a few potatoes for our supper," she begged. Reluctantly, the housewife dug a handful out of a bin and tossed them at Livia. Before long, canned pork and potatoes simmered on the stove. The travelers devoured the food in a short time.

While they were eating, their hostess wrinkled her forehead into a frown. "You refugees from the east have much more than we do," she whined. "We have not eaten such a meal in a long time." The refugees stared back at her in stunned silence.

After the meal was finished and the dishes washed, their reluctant hostess led her guests to a large cold bedroom. Everyone was so exhausted, they lay down on the bare beds in their winter coats. Livia could not sleep, but kept sniffing the air. The aroma of smoked meat seemed to come from one corner of the room. "Do you smell what I smell?" Livia whispered to Lydia.

"Let's follow our noses and find out," Lydia whispered back. In the dark, the two sisters crept over to a large wardrobe. When they opened the door, a ray of moonlight illuminated an amazing sight. Instead of clothing, rows of smoked sausages, bacon and ham were hanging there. Quietly, they shut the wardrobe door.

"How could that stingy woman claim that we have better food?" Livia mumbled.

"When the Russians get here," Lydia whispered. "They will quickly relieve her of her bounty." The sisters went back to bed with visions of sausages floating through their dreams. Leaving that unfriendly place was not difficult on the following morning.

Although they had been traveling endlessly, Livia and Lydia had kept track of the days. On the night of Feb. 13, 1945, they stayed in a small settlement near the city of Dresden.

While the others went to sleep in a house, Lydia stayed on the wagon to guard it. During the night, she was jarred awake by a loud blast. The back end of the wagon lifted off the ground as the earth shook. One explosion followed another. Quivering with fright, Lydia cautiously lifted the flap of the canopy. The sky over Dresden flashed with brilliant red lights that looked like Christmas trees. Bright lights blinded her eyes, as bombs dropped out of the sky. In the distance, flames leaped up into the night." Oh God, have mercy on us!" Lydia screamed into the darkness.

Wrapping her coat tightly around her, Lydia crept out of the wagon. She slithered close to the ground toward the house. Each bomb blast shook her body violently. At last, she stumbled through the door, right into Livia's open arms. "Thank God, you are not hurt," Livia's tears mingled with Lydia's as they clung to each other. "I was so worried about you when the bombing started. I was standing by the door, praying, when I heard you creep up."

"Just think what would have happened to us if we had gone to Dresden like we had planned to do previously," Lydia gasped out with quivering lips.

"We have been spared an awful fate." Livia wrung her hands. "By traveling with the captain and his group, we avoided death."

"Thank God! Thank God!" Lydia's voice echoed down the hall. While the bombing continued, the two sisters clung to each other. Finally, a deathly silence filled the air.

As soon as it dawned, the captain ordered everyone to get ready to leave, within half an hour. Although they were twenty—eight kilometers from Dresden, terrible devastation marked every place. A cloud of black smoke billowed into the sky above the city. Their route took them through a scene that was worse than the most terrible nightmare. Charred bodies, the size of dolls and twisted body parts littered the countryside. Blackened beams and other burning debris lay strewn about in ragged heaps. "Stay inside the wagon and don't look out!" Livia warned. Her own eyes overflowed with tears. Her stomach churned violently. It heaved, until Livia retched over the side of the wagon. Man's inhumanity to man was beyond comprehension. Why was this happening? Livia believed in God. How could He allow such cruelty to go on? The dreadful carnage shook her faith to the core.

Even as her eyes looked upon the devastation, Livia never comprehended what had really happened. Over 90% of the city center had been destroyed. During the night, four Allied bomber raids had dropped thousands of bombs and incendiary devices on the city of Dresden. By targeting the center of the city, they hoped to disrupt transportation, destroy stores of munitions and damage industries involved in the war effort. To assist the Soviet advance from the east, the Allies wanted to cause confusion among German troops and refugees. Their efforts helped to crush what was left of the German morale.

At last, late in the day, the refugees on the wagon left the disaster behind. Livia sat beside the driver in a daze. She felt as if she had passed through hell. When she tried to fall asleep that night, images of charred bodies appeared before her eyes. She thrashed about, trying to erase the horrible visions. Desperately, she cried out to God for peace. Finally, she drifted off into a troubled sleep.

The next day their trek went on. They reached a bridge crossing the Elbe River about mid- morning. Soldiers stood guard in front of it. Only military vehicles and personnel were allowed to cross. Led by the captain and his sergeant, the covered wagon rolled across unhindered, in the middle of the military column. How thankful the refugees were for their companions!

For over three weeks, the "gypsies" had been on the road. By now, they fervently longed for a place to stay. Nerves were so raw that they started to snap. Grandmother Emma could no longer move. Gerda carried her stiff mother on and off the wagon every day. The children, especially Dagmar, grew restless. She squirmed and jumped up and down, annoying Grandmother Emma. "Can't you do something to keep that child still?" the old woman whimpered. "She is giving me a headache." Aunt Lydia, who sat beside the child, was frustrated. What could she do?

"If you don't sit still, the goose will bite you," she threatened and pinched Dagmar lightly. The little girl winced, moved over and sat still for a while.

Livia stared blankly ahead. She had no energy left to deal with her children. One wish consumed her. 'Please, let us find a place to call home.'

That evening, the travelers reached a village overrun with refugees. No accommodation was available. The captain and Livia went from house to house. Finally, they found room at the inn. The weary family dozed, leaning against one another on wooden benches. Only the children could stretch out across their laps.

In the morning they could barely move, but they had to travel on. Weariness overtook them and their heads nodded as the wagon clattered along. After a long day, they arrived at the little village of *Goellnitz*, district *Thuringia*. The burgomaster of the place opened his home to them. How thankful the refugees were for a hot meal and a proper place to sleep!

Livia approached the kind mayor at breakfast the next morning. "*Herr* Winkler," she said politely. "Is it possible for our family to remain here in your village? We are so tired of roaming the earth."

The mayor scratched his head and thought for a few minutes. "I am required to take in a quota of refugees," he replied. "But to get official permission, you must apply to the district supervisor, *Frau* Braun.

"Would you kindly take me to see her?" Livia pleaded. She placed the last bottle of vodka on his desk.

"Yes, we'll go over to her house as soon as I finish a little business" The burgomaster grabbed the liquor, nodded his head and smiled. Livia looked joyfully at her loved ones. Could it be true? She hoped that their request would be granted.

Within an hour, Herr Winkler and Livia stood before *Frau* Braun. She was a kind- looking lady with crinkly gray hair pulled back into a bun. "What can I do for you?" she asked.

"My family and I request permission to reside in this village," Livia said politely. She tried to keep her trembling hands still. "We are refugees from Poland and have been traveling for over three weeks." Livia handed the woman their identification papers. The district supervisor carefully inspected the papers.

"Please sit down for a few minutes while I check my records," the lady pointed Livia to an empty chair. She opened a large book on her desk.

"I believe these people are honest," interjected the mayor. "They will not be a burden to us."

After *Frau* Braun had scanned the list of village residents, she looked up. "Yes, I do believe we have two places available." She smiled at Livia. " Your sisters and your mother can stay in a room above the inn, where *Frau* Brautigam is the mistress. You, *Frau* Falk, and your children, will reside at the home of the widow Krueger. I will inform these ladies to expect you." The woman rose from her desk and extended her hand to Livia. "Welcome to *Goellnitz*," she said.

"*Vielen Dank!*" exclaimed Livia almost jumping for joy. "And may God bless you!"

What excitement filled everyone when they heard the good news! *Goellnitz* would be their new home. They could hardly believe it. The mayor directed the wagon driver to each residence. Bundles and suitcases had to be sorted out at every place.

Lydia, Gerda and Grandmother Emma climbed the stairs to the second story above the inn. When their new landlady opened the door to the room, the three women gasped. Inside stood a single and a double bed, a wardrobe, a table, three chairs and a small stove with two burners. White lace curtains hung across the window. This room was meant for them! When Grandmother Emma finally realized that she could stay, she burst into tears.

"My God," she cried. "You have had mercy on an old woman. I will never stop praising You."

The next stop was the home of the Widow Krueger. A small, gray-haired woman welcomed her new family. She led them to a large bedroom at the back of the house. It was equipped with two beds and a child's crib. A small dresser, a wardrobe and two chairs filled one corner of the room. Two large windows covered with white curtains, looked out over the garden. "This is your bedroom," said *Frau* Krueger. "You will have to share the sitting room and kitchen facilities with me."

"Thank you, very much." Livia choked back tears of joy. Frank looked around the house in awe, while Dagmar bounced up and down with excitement. They had found a home at last.

CHAPTER 8

To get over the sad experiences of that winter, the refugees delighted themselves in their new home. The picturesque, little village lay deep in a valley, surrounded by hills. Only the church tower was visible from the approaching highway. When spring arrived, the fruit trees decked themselves in delicate blossoms. New life surged, not only in nature, but also in the hearts of those who had lost so much and come so far.

On Sundays, they went for long walks, absorbing all the freshness around them. It was an eight—kilometer distance to the nearest church. When it became warm enough, they carried their shoes, in order to save them, until they reached the town. They were glad to worship and fellowship with others once again. Only Grandmother Emma was too weak to make that journey.

In the early spring of 1945, war still raged in the surrounding area, but so far *Goellnitz* had been spared. The only signs of fighting were swarms of bombers swooping overhead. On a hillside, beyond the village, stood an anti-aircraft gun. It had never been used until one night.

Violent cannon fire woke Livia from her sleep. She bolted from her bed and looked out the window. Brilliant flashes of light illuminated the night sky. "Not this again!" Livia moaned. All hope of sleep was gone. Who was attacking them, now?

The next morning, the shooting had stopped. Livia held her breath. Would peaceful *Goellnitz* become a war zone? Around mid-morning, a cry echoed from house to house. "They are coming!" The villagers hid in the safety of their homes and peeked cautiously from behind their curtains. Soon, a row of tanks, followed by khaki-clad soldiers, rolled down the hillside, onto the main street of the village. The 'Stars and Stripes' floated above them in the morning breeze— Americans!

Livia, who had also been watching, heaved a sigh of relief. "Thank God!" she exclaimed and hugged her children. "We have been occupied by the Americans and not the Russians." She grabbed her children by their hands and ran outside. Her joy was reflected in the faces of all the others who watched the liberators march in. Children plucked wild flowers from the roadside and showered the soldiers with these blossoms. *Goellnitz* had not seen such a celebration in a long time.

Everyone realized that the war was finally over. Those who owned a radio soon heard the monumental news. On May 8, 1945, Germany officially capitulated and signed its surrender to the Allies. A rumor circulated that Hitler and his mistress had committed suicide, but no one really knew the truth. Most Germans were happy that peace had come at last to their devastated country.

As yet, no word had arrived from Eduard or Bruno. Livia and Lydia wondered about the fate of their husbands. After all, their men had no way of knowing if they were alive, either. The uncertainty weighed heavily upon the hearts and minds of the women.

When summer arrived, Lydia decided to stop worrying and find a useful occupation. She joined the ranks of other women who went to work in the fields. With a hoe in hand, she began the unfamiliar task of hacking out weeds. Aches and pains tormented her body, but she kept on. At the end of the summer, she even helped with the threshing. The extra produce and grain that she earned from her labors, were a big help to the rest of the family.

Meager food rations were doled out to each refugee family by the means of coupons. With the additional vegetables, Lydia, Gerda and their mother would not go hungry. Lydia also gave generous portions to Livia and the children. Except for a shortage of fat and meat, they ate quite well.

After the sugar beet harvest, the refugees learned another skill from the locals. They chopped sugar beets and cooked them into a mush. Then, the women strained that through a cloth and boiled down the resulting liquid into thick, dark syrup. What a treat it was to spread sweet syrup on their heavy, rye bread!

Living in *Goellnitz* was quite enjoyable until one day, when everything changed. Without warning, the American forces withdrew from the village and Russian soldiers marched in.

Now, Livia and her family were under the control of the Soviets, from whom they had been escaping. What would happen to her and her family, now?

Life under the new masters was quite different. Although the Russians could no longer engage in wartime atrocities, they made their presence felt in other ways. Under the Communist system all properties belonged to the state. They quickly dispossessed farmers of their land. The villagers quaked in silent fear of what the Russians would do next.

Communication with the Russian officials was nearly impossible. When *Frau* Krueger discovered that Livia could speak Russian, she was overjoyed. "Please come with me and be my interpreter. I need to settle things about my property."

Reluctantly, Livia agreed to go with *Frau* Krueger to see the Russian officer. She would have never done this if *Frau* Krueger had not been so kind to her and the children. On the way to the town hall, Livia took Frank and Dagmar for a visit to their aunts and grandmother. At the hall, Livia and *Frau* Kruger sat on hard wooden benches in the waiting room. The two women waited a long time before a soldier ushered them into the commandant's office.

"*Guten Tag*," the Russian officer mumbled in heavily accented German, without raising his eyes from the papers in front of him. "And what is your business with me?"

Frau Krueger was intimidated by his gruff tone. After Livia repeated his question into her ear, the woman stepped forward. "Here is the deed to my house and lands," she stammered. "I will surrender my lands to you, if you will let me keep my house. It has been in my family for generations." *Frau* Krueger dropped her precious document on the man's desk. She stepped back while Livia interpreted her words into Russian.

Suddenly, the commandant raised his head and stared at Livia. His deep-set, blue eyes gazed into her brown ones. A gasp escaped from Livia's lips. She had seen that look before. Narrowing her eyes, she squinted, searching his face. It couldn't be . . .

The commandant seemed to have lost track of the business at hand. He stamped the paper and handed it back to *Frau* Krueger. "Your request is granted," he said brusquely. His eyes still rested on Livia. Dismissing *Frau* Krueger with a wave of his hand, he arose and asked Livia to stay. Her throat went dry as *Frau* Krueger shut the door behind her. The commandant cleared the space between them in one bound. "Are you someone I knew long ago?" he asked. "Are you Livia Dust?"

At the sound of her maiden name, Livia's eyes widened. "Yes, I am Livia," she whispered. Her throat felt so tight. "And you must be Sergei Ivanoff. I hardly recognized you."

Suddenly, Livia's legs gave way and she nearly fell. A strong arm grabbed her and steered her to a nearby chair.

"Livia!" Sergei's voice shook with emotion. "Is it possible that we meet again after so many years? You have not changed very much. How did you get here, so far from your old home?"

"Oh Sergei," Livia gasped. "It is such a long story. I am married now, with a husband and two children. We had to flee when your armies overran our homeland."

"I am so sorry!" Sergei exclaimed sincerely. "I will not detain you any longer. But, I must see you again. Please, tell me exactly where you live." Reluctantly, Livia told Sergei where *Frau* Kruger's house was located. "I would like to come to visit you tomorrow evening," Segei went on.

"I will have to think about that," replied Livia. "For now, it has been enough to see you again." Slowly, she rose from the chair and grasped the doorknob. She turned and looked at Sergei again. "Until tomorrow, perhaps," she blurted out and was gone.

Outside of the office, *Frau* Krueger was still waiting. She raised big, questioning eyes. Vainly, Livia fumbled around for an explanation. "He wanted to ask me more questions,"

When she was alone that evening, after her children were asleep, a battle raged in Livia's mind. How handsome Sergei looked with his clipped mustache! He still seemed to care about her. She wondered how Communist ideology had influenced Sergei. Then, Livia thought about Eduard involved in the war against the Russians. Even though they did not love each other, he was still her husband. Perhaps, he was injured or not even alive any more? Livia tossed and turned in bed. Sleep did not come for a long time.

CHAPTER 9

What turmoil filled Livia's heart during the next day! She tried to hide her agitation from her children or her sisters. On the one hand, she longed to be with Sergei. On the other hand, his offer went against all her Christian principles. In confusion, she opened her Bible at random.

Her eyes scanned the page. The words jumped out at her, 'You cannot serve two masters'.

Livia's conscience pricked her. How could she go against her marriage vows? Yet, the battle in her heart raged all day long.

Before the evening meal, Livia had reached her decision. She ran to Lydia's place and asked her to stay with the children that evening. "The Russian officer, for whom I interpreted, wants to visit me," she told her sister. "I can't face him again."

When Lydia came to *Frau* Krueger's house, Livia drifted away down the shadowed lane. "I am staying with Wanda Gerandt," she whispered over her shoulder. "I hope all will be well with you and the children."

While she served the food to her nephew and niece, Lydia kept on peeking out of the window. Before long, she saw the Russian officer coming down the street. He was carrying a sack on his shoulders. Lydia lifted Dagmar into her arms and went to the garden gate. "*Guten Abend*," said Sergei in stilted German. "*Wo ist Frau* Falk?"

Lydia shrugged her shoulders. "She is not at home," she answered.

"I come for a little visit and bring food," the man went on. Lydia shook her head.

"Please, I want to see *Frau* Falk," the Russian pleaded. Lydia shrugged her shoulders again.

"I told you. She is not home," she said and turned back to the house, with Dagmar in her arms.

"Please tell me where *Frau* Falk is," the man pleaded again. Lydia simply waved good-bye, and kept on going. In frustration, the officer turned and walked slowly back to his quarters.

When Livia returned, she knew that she had to avoid any further contact with Sergei from now on.

Next morning, she kept her thoughts at bay by plunging into a mountain of laundry. First, she scrubbed stained spots on a washboard. Then, she boiled whites and darks in separate kettles of soapy water, stirring them with a large wooden spoon. She let the pots cool, wrung out the pieces by hand and rinsed them in clean water. Finally, she carried the heavy baskets outside and began to hang her wash on the clothesline. The summer breeze would dry everything quickly.

While her mother worked, Dagmar scampered about in the garden, picking wild flowers. Frank had gone off to play with some of his friends. Livia began to hang up the sheets.

The refreshing wind cooled her hot cheeks. She gazed up into the cloudless, blue sky above. What a lovely summer day this was! 'If only my heart was not so heavy!' thought Livia.

Suddenly, she saw *Frau* Krueger hurrying around the corner of the house. She was clutching a big basket of bread and rolls that she had bought at the bakery. The lady puffed loudly. Her face was flushed and perspiration dripped from her double chin. "*Frau* Falk," she gasped.

"Come quickly out into the main street. A skeleton is stumbling towards our house. He looks like . . ." *Frau* Krueger never finished her sentence.

Livia dropped the clothespins and the sheet she was hanging, and rushed out into the street. The sight was unbelievable. Down the street, staggered Eduard, looking more dead than alive. Livia stood rooted to the spot. As Eduard came closer, he recognized his wife and waved feebly. A few minutes later, he stood before her. Livia felt his bony arms go around her, but she was unable to respond. Finally, she shook herself out of her stupor.

"Eddek," she stammered. "You look like a ghost. Come into the house and sit down." Livia led the way into the kitchen. Eduard stumbled inside, behind her and dropped onto a chair.

Frau Krueger, who had watched the whole scene, frowned. She stepped outside and called, "Dagmar! Go into the house, child." She beckoned to the little girl. "Bring your bouquet of flowers into the kitchen." Dagmar skipped lightly into the room. She stopped abruptly and stared at the strange man sitting there and guzzling down a glass of water.

"Come closer, Dagmar," Livia encouraged her daughter. "This is your father, who has been a prisoner of war for a long time." Shyly, the daughter stepped closer, examining his emaciated face. She had only a vague recollection of her father. After a few minutes, she thrust out the bouquet of flowers. "Here, these are for you," she said quickly. Eduard took the flowers and beckoned to his daughter.

"Come closer, my child." His voice sounded old and raspy. "I want to give you a hug."

Dagmar backed off and started to cry. She was frightened of this bony man. She tried to run away, but her mother stopped her.

"Dagmar, be a good girl," Livia admonished her daughter. "Give your papa a hug." She prodded the child forward. Reluctantly, Dagmar gave her father a quick hug, and darted outside to the safety of the garden.

After a while, Frank came home. Dagmar informed him who was in the house with Mother.

The boy peeked into the kitchen. His father was slurping some soup from a bowl. Frank backed off again. He didn't want to meet his father, yet. He was old enough to remember him, but his memories were not very good.

Meanwhile, Livia led her husband to the bedroom. He certainly needed a good rest. After he fell asleep, she returned to the kitchen and called the children in for lunch. She hardly knew how to answer their questions.

"Why is he so skinny?" asked Dagmar.

"He did not get enough food in prison camp," answered her mother.

"How long will he be staying?" Frank wanted to know.

"He is your father," Livia replied. "From now on, he will always stay with us."

"Will he get a job?" Dagmar was curious.

"Right now, he needs to get his strength back." Livia tried to be patient with all the questions. "After he feels better, we will see."

"We were better off without him," concluded Frank, and dashed off to play again.

"Don't say that!" Livia shouted after him. She was thankful that *Frau* Krueger was in her own room and had not heard this last remark. Deep in her heart, Livia knew it was true.

What would life be like for them, now? Quietly, she washed the lunch dishes and then, went out to finish hanging the laundry. She was worn out from the morning's events. While Dagmar played close by, Livia rested on a garden bench, staring vaguely into space.

Her world had been turned upside down. She had no choice but to take care of her ailing husband. How she dreaded the inevitable! Tears trickled down her cheeks. She wiped them away with her handkerchief. Crying would not help. She had to be strong and hide her worries.

While Eduard was resting the next morning, Livia took Dagmar by the hand and went to tell the news to her sisters and her mother. She hoped she would not meet Sergei anywhere.

"Yesterday morning, something totally unexpected happened," Livia told her sisters in a quaking voice. "Yesterday, Eddek returned home from prison camp." Her sisters stared at her open-mouthed.

"Are you telling us that Eduard is back?" Lydia finally asked. "How is it possible that he survived prison camp?"

"He is only barely alive." Livia squirmed in her seat. "To make a long story short, I must take care of him. He is in terrible physical condition." Her sisters and her mother were momentarily lost for words. Livia rose and walked to the door. "I have to go," she stammered."

Her sisters came out of their daze. "Don't leave yet, Livia," Lydia pleaded. "How will you manage?"

"I'm not sure," answered Livia. "I will have to take life one day at a time."

"We will do whatever we can to help you," added Gerda.

"I know that I can depend on both of you," Livia replied. "With God's help, I will do my best for Eddek and the children." As Livia plodded home, she knew that she must absolutely forget about Sergei, and what might have been.

CHAPTER 10

Ever since her husband's return, Livia's life had fallen into a dull routine. She arose early each morning, made a fire in the kitchen stove and prepared breakfast as best she could. She was waiting for extra coupons, to get Eddek's portion of the allotted rations. Without a drop of fat on hand, Livia toasted a handful of flour in a pan and added water to make gruel. This was supplemented by a little skim milk. Fortunately, she still had sugar beet syrup to spread on their dark, rye bread. When breakfast was ready, she called the rest of the family into the kitchen."Do I have to eat that?" Dagmar screwed up her face and pushed the gruel away.

"Take a few mouthfuls at least," her mother coaxed. The child swallowed a mouthful and gagged.

"Eat what your mother has prepared." Eduard looked sternly at his daughter. She managed to choke down a few more spoonfuls. Her father gulped his own gruel. On this meager diet he would not gain weight or get much stronger.

Frank refused to taste the gruel. Instead, he took a thin slice of bread, spread on a little syrup and ate that. Then, he swallowed a glass of blue-tinted, skim milk. "I have to leave for school," he said, rising from his chair. "May I be excused?"

"Oh Frank!" Livia looked anxiously at her son. "You hardly ate enough. How will you be able to learn with so little in your stomach?"

"Don't worry, Mother." Frank hoisted his satchel onto his back and sprinted towards the door. "I'll be home for lunch."

Right after breakfast, Livia prepared soup for lunch. She was grateful for the vegetables she had stored in the cellar. She peeled potatoes and onions, scrubbed carrots and cored cabbage. When the water in the big pot was bubbling, she dropped in the chopped vegetables. If she only had a little meat to add, her soup would be far more nutritious. What use was it to wish for something impossible?

While her soup simmered, she started doing the rest of her chores. First, she washed the dishes. Dagmar stood on a low stool and dried them. "I am going out to play, Mommy," Dagmar announced when she was finished and skipped outside.

The iron was already heating on the hot stove. Livia started in on a pile of laundry. The hot iron hissed on a damp shirt. Beads of perspiration gathered on Livia's forehead, and her cheeks flushed. She pushed the hot iron to smooth out any wrinkles. Her strokes were automatic, while her thoughts wandered. She only wished that she could iron out her problems as easily.

With Eduard at home, their resources were stretched to the limit. Their rations allowance had increased only slightly. If her sisters had not helped out with gifts of fruit and vegetables, her family would be barely surviving. Livia wondered when Eduard would be strong enough to get a job. They needed an income—very soon.

The coming of fall turned the hills around *Goellnitz* into a spectacular tapestry of color. Not only was it a feast for the eyes, but it also brought opportunities to gather extra food for the winter. After the pickers were finished in the orchards, needy people were allowed to glean the fruit that had fallen on the ground. Livia and her sisters started gathering early in the mornings, while dew still lay on the ground.. Day after day they worked, gathering apples, prune plums and pears into large baskets. By noon hour, they proudly lugged home their heavy loads. Most of the fruit was peeled, cored, sliced and strung on lines to dry over the kitchen stove. If the women had their ration of sugar on hand, they cooked some fruit into thick jam.

After a rainfall, the hills yielded other benefits. Early in the morning, the three sisters set out, carrying pails in their hands. They wandered through the woods, looking for edible mushrooms. As children in Poland, they had learned to differentiate between good and poisonous, wild mushrooms. When their pails were full, they wandered home, singing joyfully, as they had done long ago. They cooked the best of their harvest to make a delicious supper. The rest of the mushrooms were cleaned and dried for later use.

During the summer, Lydia had been working in the fields. After the threshing was done, she was allowed to bring home as much grain as she could carry in a sack. She took the grain to the mill, and had it ground into flour. With that flour, Lydia and Livia made their own sourdough bread. They were like the squirrels storing acorns from the old oak trees. After all their hard work, the sisters had a good hoard laid aside for winter.

When the cold, damp winter weather arrived, the family spent most of their time indoors. Lydia, Gerda and Grandmother Emma often joined Livia and her family in the evening. How cozy it was to huddle close to the ceramic stove in the sitting room! *Frau* Krueger sat beside the oil lamp knitting, while one of the sisters told stories. Most of the time, they told how they had escaped from Poland. Frank sometimes grew tired of listening, but Dagmar loved to hear the stories over and over again. Aided by the nightly story-telling, the winter gradually passed.

How wonderful it was when winter finally yielded to spring! Longer daylight and warmer sunshine coaxed the villagers out of hibernation. Everyone seemed to have a new zest for life, except Grandmother Emma. She became more depressed every day. "The war is over now," she whined to her daughters. "When are we going back to our home in Poland?"

"We can never go back," answered Gerda. She usually took care of her mother. "The Russians or the Poles would kill us if we tried to return."

"That cannot be true." Emma shook her head. "We always got along well years ago. You just like it better here, and don't want to go back." No one could convince the old woman otherwise. She lived in the past.

As time went on, Emma's body and mind became even weaker. She longed to depart from this life. The hardships of the flight and the re-adjustments had taken their toll. In early spring, 1946, Grandmother Emma passed away. The villagers mourned together with the refugees who had become part of their community.

A long funeral procession wound its way to the hillside cemetery, overlooking the lovely little village. A visiting pastor conducted a short, meaningful graveside service. The family said their last farewell. Grandmother Emma was home at last. As Livia lingered at the graveside, she remembered how elaborate funerals had been when she was a child. In those days, the church brass band, playing mournful airs, preceded the horse-drawn hearse. Livia and her sisters had often followed behind, crying loudly with the official mourners. Now, they were far from their childhood, weeping for the loss of their mother.

When the days of mourning were over, Livia had to attend to pressing issues. As the weather turned warmer, Eduard's physical condition improved. He sat outside, soaking up the sun and developed a healthy-looking tan. Livia encouraged him to apply for any vacancies in their clergy. Many churches in their denomination had lost pastors during the war. Surely, Eduard could fill one of these spots. After several negative replies, he finally received a letter asking him to come to the city of Jena, to try out for the position of assistant pastor.

Travel by train to Jena was too expensive for both Eduard and Livia. He would have to go alone, but Livia made sure that he was adequately prepared. Every night, after the children were in bed, Livia listened to Eduard's sermon and offered suggestions to help him stay on his topic. The day before his trip, she packed his best suit, shirt and some underwear, and made a lunch for the journey. Then, she prayed fervently that he would find favor with the congregation.

After three days, Eduard returned with a smile on his face. The congregation had voted to accept him as their assistant pastor. They had even advanced a generous amount of money to enable him to make the move.

Mixed emotions surged through Livia's heart as she began to pack. She looked forward to living in this city where her husband would actually be earning a living. Yet, she was reluctant to leave the village that had become her home. So many people were now dear friends! Her beloved sisters would also stay behind. Livia even thought of Sergei. Shaking her head, she determined to forget about him.

On the day of the move, a kind neighbor, who owned a wagon, loaded up their baggage. He would take everything to the train station for them. Then, Livia said a tearful goodbye to *Frau* Krueger. Lydia and Gerda accompanied the family to the train station. On the platform, they hugged each other and hardly wanted to let go. Eduard was pacing back and forth, impatiently. The train was leaving in a few minutes. At the last minute, the Falk family tore away from their relatives and climbed into the waiting passenger car. They found seats near a window. As the train started to chug out of the station, the children waved to their aunts until the figures faded into the distance..

After several hours, the train pulled into the terminal at Jena. When Eduard, Livia and the children descended, a crushing crowd of people engulfed them. Eduard gripped his suitcase,

Livia held tightly onto Dagmar's hand, while Frank sauntered along behind them. The parents craned their necks, looking for someone to welcome them. In the distance, they saw a red handkerchief waving. A small man and his heavy-set wife were pushing through the crowd toward them. They met near the exit of the train station.

"Welcome to Jena, Brother and Sister Falk," said the little man in a high squeaky voice. Frank began to snicker, but quickly covered his mouth when he saw his mother frown.

"We are the Muellers." The corpulent lady reached out her hand. Her voice boomed. "We have come to take you to your new dwelling. Come with me." She grabbed Livia's arm and steered her outside. The others followed obediently. An open, horse-drawn carriage was waiting for them. Soon, everyone was settled on the wooden seats. The little man took the reins, clicked his tongue and the horse clip-clopped along.

The sights and sounds of the city were overwhelming. Vehicles and people streamed in opposite directions down the narrow streets. Tall buildings overshadowed the pavement. A car horn honked, a motorcycle sputtered and voices echoed. At a busy corner, a policeman's whistle directed the traffic. To the children from the country, this city was fascinating and frightening at the same time.

After a short drive, the carriage stopped in front of a tall, brown brick building. It had a fancy carved front door and an intricate roofline. Squeezing in on both sides were similar buildings.

"This is your new home," the little man squeaked. He jumped down from the driver's seat and helped his passengers descend. Then, he unloaded their hand baggage.

"Thank you for bringing us here," said Livia and pressed a coin into his hand.

"Oh, no, thank you!" The man shook his head. "I was glad to be of service." He and his wife waved goodbye to the Falk family, and got back onto their carriage.

Just then, the front door of the brown house opened. Out stepped two elderly ladies. One was tall and thin, with gray hair pulled back tightly into a bun on top of her head. The other one was short and round, with frizzy, reddish hair, bouncing out from a French roll. Both ladies stretched out their hands and smiled.

"How happy we are that you have arrived safely!" said the tall one. "My name is *Frau* Katherine Roth. This is my sister, *Frau* Meta Friederich. We are both widows and have been living together for a long time."

Eduard and Livia shook hands with the ladies. Dagmar peeked out from behind her Mother's skirt, while Frank stood aside, scrutinizing their new landladies. Then, Eduard introduced his family. "This is my wife, Livia, my son, Frank, and my daughter, Dagmar," he said. "Of course, you have met me at the church already."

The newcomers were quickly ushered into the house. *Frau* Katherine took them to the large bedroom, which would be their private quarters. The Falk family dropped their coats on a bed and set their suitcases in a corner. Then, *Frau* Katherine led them back to the sitting room. Meanwhile, *Frau* Meta had been bustling about in the kitchen. As soon as everyone was seated, she came out carrying a large tray. She handed cups of tea to the adults, glasses of milk to the children and then, passed open-face sandwiches to everyone.

The hungry travelers devoured every morsel and thanked their hostesses. What a kind welcome they had received!

The day after they arrived, Eduard hired a wagon to pick up the rest of their belongings from the train depot. Livia left the children with their landladies and came along. She wanted to be sure that they got everything that they had sent. At the depot, they found a worker to unlock the freight car. He shoved open the metal door and plunged into the dim interior. Quickly, he jumped back again. "It is empty!" he exclaimed.

"That is impossible," shouted Eduard. "Our belongings were locked inside when the train left *Goellnitz*."

"Well, look for yourselves." The man backed off and wrinkled his forehead. Both Eduard and Livia looked inside the dark freight car. It was empty, just like the man had said. They could not believe their eyes. The sturdy wooden crates containing their dishes, pots and pans were gone. The bundle of their pillows and featherbeds had vanished. Even their large suitcases had disappeared. Livia and Eduard were numb with shock.

"No one tampered with this lock before I opened it." The young worker tried to apologize. "Someone must have broken in before this train left *Goellnitz*. Sorry for your loss."

Livia stumbled backward, feeling faint. Eduard caught her just in time. "Who could have done this?" he asked in dismay.

"Everything is gone!" Livia blubbered. "They even stole the few things we rescued out of Poland." She covered her face and wept uncontrollably.

"Crying won't bring anything back." Eduard looked perplexed. "God will provide for us. Come, let us go back to our new place." Livia offered no resistance but walked stiffly to the wagon. Their only belongings were the clothes on their backs and the few things they had brought in the small suitcases.

When they got back to their new residence, Livia could hardly face their children or the two landladies. "All our belongings have been stolen," she stammered. "We have nothing- nothing at all."

"That is terrible!" *Frau* Friederich shook her head. Her kind face puckered up with concern. "We will see to it that you will be looked after."

"Yes, please don't worry!" the tall sister clenched her jaw and put her hands on her hips. "Try to relax and leave the rest to us."

The two women were as good as their word. In a short time they spread the word to other members of the congregation. In spite of post-war shortages, an outpouring of generosity followed. In the next few days, one church member after another came to the house bearing gifts. They brought clothing, pots and pans, odd dishes, bedding and anything else they could spare. Soon, Livia and Eduard had to tell them to stop. The only things that could not be replaced were family keepsakes and photos.

CHAPTER 11

When fall of that year arrived, the Falk family had almost forgotten their loss and begun to enjoy life in the big city. Jena was located on the *Saale* River, in the heart of *Thuringia.*

Destinations, such as the Planetarium or the *Zeiss* Company grounds, were interesting places to visit. All around the city, lovely hills ascended from the valley. On one of these hills, stood an ancient tower, surrounded by thick walls, that were once part of a fortress. It was a favorite spot for Sunday afternoon outings. Livia and the children gladly hiked out into the countryside, but Eduard found the exercise too strenuous.

In Jena, the Falk family enjoyed life, except for the continuing food rationing. Whenever possible, Livia took the children along to obtain necessary supplies. She sent Frank off with a coupon to wait in a long queue at the bakery. Dagmar was now old enough to stand in line at the milk vendor's, while Livia waited patiently in front of the butcher's store. She hoped that she would still be able to get their one-pound allotment of meat. How thankful she was for the blessings, which her sisters brought when they came to visit! Instead of clothing, their suitcases were packed with dried fruit, syrup, or even baked goods. Whenever the aunts came to visit, the Falk family celebrated by eating delicacies they could not obtain in the city.

By now, Eduard and Liva had settled comfortably into the church community. Eduard's sermons went fairly well, after coaxing and rehearsals. When he wandered off the topic, Livia clenched her hands and broke out into a cold sweat. She tried to signal him with her eyes, to draw out his closing words. During the week, Eduard complemented his rambling by spending long hours visiting church members. Eduard loved to talk—loud and long. Often, Livia had to nudge him to quit, before his monologue became too embarrassing.

One drawback of being a church pastor was the fact that Eduard and Livia had to spend nights at prolonged church meetings. Livia hated having to leave the children alone in their huge bedroom. Colorful baroque paintings decorated the ceiling. The figures were very interesting in daylight, but frightening at night. In the moonlight, the figures seemed to come alive and dance about. Frank fell peacefully asleep, but Dagmar hid under her covers. She could not sleep until her parents entered the bedroom. "Mommy," she whimpered. "Come and hold me. Those figures are trying to grab me."

"*Sei still, mein Liebling*," her mother soothed. "They are only paintings on the ceiling. Please, go to sleep." As Livia rocked her daughter, the child's eyes closed. When she was asleep, the mother could also relax.

Livia soon discovered the source of the fear. Their landladies, *Frau* Katherine and *Frau* Meta were very superstitious and told ghost stories until late in the evening. Many years before, they had absorbed occult ideas while living in Brazil. They had both been young brides when their husbands decided to leave Germany. During the severe economic depression in their homeland, Brazil beckoned as a land of opportunity. The couples had lived and prospered in that far-away place. When both husbands died from influenza, their wives returned to their old home in Germany. They intended to stay only long enough to sell their property. Before they had a chance to go back to Brazil, the Second World War broke out. They were trapped. In their old home, they carried on the occult practices they had learned in Brazil. Even though their church frowned on such things, the sisters held séances and believed in the existence of ghosts.

At night, after supper, Eduard, Livia and the children usually joined the two sisters in the sitting room. One of the two elderly women soon started telling about supernatural occurrences. She pulled out a yellowed letter, written in faded handwriting, from the bureau drawer. Supposedly, it had been sent from paradise by their youngest, deceased sister. *Frau* Katherine insisted on reading the letter.

'My Dear Loved Ones On Earth,
    I am living in such a beautiful place. Everything is perfect here. I wander through a delightful garden or sit beside a sparkling pool. I feel no sorrow and cry no more tears. How I wish that you could be with me!

Longing to see you again,
Your sister, Susanne.'

Eduard and Livia believed in heaven, but to receive a letter from there was doubtful. Neither of the ladies was dissuaded by their skepticism. Katherine insisted upon proving the reality of their ethereal visitors. She launched into another tale about their uncle. He had been a bachelor and had died years ago in the very bedroom that the Falk family now occupied. Whenever he became lonely for his sisters, he floated down from heaven, through the bedroom window and right into this room. Both Katherine and Meta had seen him.

Frank and Dagmar listened, spellbound, to this story. Imagine – the old uncle might be floating in through their window right now! "That's enough story telling for tonight," announced Livia.

She rose, took Dagmar's hand and walked out. No wonder her daughter was so frightened when she had to stay in that bedroom, while her parents were at a church meeting.

How Livia longed for another place where they could spend their evenings! She hated to offend her kind hostesses, but she had to protect her children from the ghost stories. Livia determined to find a way to prove once and for all that ghosts did not exist.

One evening, Eduard was away at a church business meeting. He had forgotten to take his key. Livia was reading a book, while she waited for him in the sitting room. She did not realize how late it was until the clock struck twelve. Livia listened, hoping to hear Eduard's knock. Instead, she heard a distinct rustle in the corner, beside the stove. She got up to investigate. It was only crunched up paper in the wastebasket, uncurling from the heat. Livia sat down again. She stared at the French doors leading into the dining room. The doors were moving back and forth. Livia thought that her weary eyes were playing tricks. She got up and shut the doors firmly. When she sat down again, the doors seemed to be moving. Livia broke out in a cold sweat. She rose and checked the doors. They were closed. When she sat down and looked again, they were swinging on their hinges.

Livia would not allow herself to be sucked into a pit of fear. She closed her eyes tight and began to pray. When she opened them, the doors stood still. Her heart beat so loudly, that she hardly heard Eduard's knock on the outside door. She hurried down the steps to open it.

How glad she was to leave that room! She pulled the covers over her head that night.

From that time on, Livia tried to steer the landladies away from frightening stories. Of course, that was nearly impossible. Meanwhile, she began to look for another residence, away from unseen apparitions. Before that could happen, another bit of news changed everything.

For some time already, Eduard and Livia had sensed increased pressure from the Communist government of East Germany. State edicts began to curtail the spread of religion. Times and lengths of church services were regulated. Rumors abounded about the sudden disappearance of church ministers. The assistant minister and his wife were very careful not to express any anti-communist sentiments. They never knew if an informer was listening. Secretly, they wondered what the future held.

In the spring of 1948, Livia went as usual to get her mail. She leafed through the bundle to find a letter from Lydia. It had been opened and censored. Then, Livia saw another unopened envelope, bearing an official looking seal. Livia hurried to the sitting room to read her mail.

First, she wanted to read the letter from her sister. Lydia had exciting news from the Red Cross. The organization had located her husband, Bruno. He was still a prisoner in Siberia, but would soon be allowed to contact his wife. What good news after so many years!

Next, Livia tore open the mysterious envelope. She spread out the sheet of paper, and saw that it came from a good friend who worked in the municipal offices of Jena. Quickly, Livia scanned the lines.

> "Dear Livia,
>
> I hope that you and your family are in good health. In the course of my work, I have come across information of importance to you. I found a list of persons who are designated for labor in the coalmines of Siberia. Your husband, Eduard is on that list. In one month, our government intends to send him to do 'real work'. I know, from what you told me in the past, that he would not survive those brutal conditions. If he is wise, he will disappear before then.
>
> My best wishes to you and the children. I hope that your plans will succeed. Please burn this letter after you have read it.
>
> Your loving friend,
> Johanna."

Livia's hands trembled as she read and reread the letter. She folded it and put it back in the envelope. Then, she lifted her eyes to heaven. "Thank you God, for this warning," she prayed. She clutched the letter to her heart and hurried to their bedroom. She thrust it into the stove and then, went to tell Eduard the bad news.

That night, after the children were asleep, Livia and Eduard talked in hushed tones. "My only hope is to escape to the West," Eduard stated. "I will find a reason to visit other churches in our district. In the process, I will proceed closer to the border."

"Ask our most trusted friends about the safest route," Livia added. "You must get away as soon as possible. In the meantime, the rest of us must avoid suspicion."

Eduard and Livia bowed their heads and prayed for God's guidance and protection. Then, they began to plan the escape.

Chapter 12

How difficult it was to act unconcerned during the day, when the evenings were filled with clandestine activity! Secretly, Eduard made contact with a Christian man who would guide him across the border. He wound up his church business and prepared for his extended visit.

Livia packed only essential items into his rucksack, so that he would not be weighed down.

The parents did not tell the children anything, until just before Eduard's departure.

After supper, the family relaxed as usual in the sitting room. *Frau* Katherine smiled happily at her audience and started another one of her stories. The children were enthralled, but Livia and Eduard squirmed in their seats. "I think it is time to get the children to bed," Livia covered a yawn. "I feel rather tired myself."

"Already?" Katherine stopped in the middle of her tale. "It is much too early to go to bed."

"That may be true," answered Eduard. "But we have had a busy day, and I need to be up early tomorrow." He rose from his soft chair.

"Please let us hear the end of the story," Frank pleaded.

"Well, we will hear the end, but then, we must leave." His father sat back down. As soon as Katherine had finished, the Falk family said, "*Gute Nacht*," and went to their bedroom.

When they had shut the door, the parents pulled their children beside them, onto the big bed.

"We have something important to tell you," said Eduard in a hushed voice. He coughed and his eyes watered. He could not go on.

"Your father must leave us tonight," Livia continued where he had left off. "His life is in danger. Our communist government wants to do away with ministers of the gospel."

"Where is he going?" Dagmar wanted to know.

"He will try to get to West Germany," Livia said in a shaky voice. "We don't know exactly where, yet."

"Isn't it dangerous to escape?" asked Frank, who understood the situation better.

"Yes, it is very dangerous." Livia clasped and unclasped her hands. "But your father must go before a worse fate befalls him."

"What worse fate?" asked Dagmar in a shaky voice.

"I am designated to work in a coal mine in Siberia," her father said softly. "It is not likely that I would survive those harsh conditions." A heavy silence fell as the children tried to comprehend the news. "You must not breathe a word about this to anyone." Eduard warned. "By tomorrow morning, I will be on my way. Your mother will explain to our landladies."

"Let us bow our heads and pray for God's protection." Livia grasped both children's hands and folded them into her own. Together, the family uttered fervent prayers for Eduard's safety and success on this escape.

Uncertainty plagued Livia during the following days and weeks. She went about her business as usual, but secretly, she wondered if

Eduard had made it. By this time, the church members knew of his escape, but everyone kept quiet. Sometimes, Livia had to answer official questions regarding her husband's whereabouts. She stuck to the story of his visit to faraway churches. How long would she be able to keep up this charade?

Meanwhile, worries about her children overwhelmed Livia. Frank became more and more independent in his thinking. He fought against having to attend church. What would become of this stubborn boy? On top of that, came concerns about Dagmar. She caught one childhood illness after another. She had started school, but now, had to miss so much because of sickness. With the reduction of Eduard's portion of food rations, Livia could not provide the nourishment that her daughter needed to get better. Oh, what could she do?

After weeks of waiting and wondering, Livia received a short note from the West. The letter had been opened and censored, but thankfully, Eduard had written in code. 'The back pack and bearer arrived safely at the address below. Require response ASAP. E.F., Hanover, West Germany,' it said. This was the clue for her and the children to come to Hanover.

Secretly, Livia began to plan the next phase of the escape. That day, she wrote to the same people who had helped her husband. She warned Frank and Dagmar to keep quiet about their plans. Quietly, she sold any possessions that could not be carried in backpacks or suitcases. These goods would go to close friends or church members. They could not be picked up, until after she and the children had gone.

By mid fall of 1948, Livia had everything arranged. She informed her landladies of the plan, but asked them to keep quiet. Shortly afterwards, Lydia arrived to help them during the journey. Gerda had decided to stay back in *Goellnitz* for the time being, so that the people there would not get suspicious.

When the day of departure had finally arrived, and they were ready to leave the house, Dagmar lingered behind in the sitting room. She looked fondly at the dolls that she had played with. They belonged to the two elderly ladies. *Frau* Meta saw the longing in Dagmar's eyes. "You may take one along," she said.

Just as Dagmar reached for her favorite doll, Livia entered the room. She put her arms around the child and pulled her away. "*Oh mein Liebling.*" Livia had difficulty getting out the words. "You cannot take that doll."

"Why not, Mommy?" Dagmar turned and wrinkled her forehead.

"A doll could be a real drawback on our perilous journey," her mother explained. "If you were to drop it during our border crossing, you might cry out and give us all away."

"Oh Mommy, I won't drop it." The little girl started to cry.

"We cannot take such a chance," her mother said firmly, trying to hide the tears in her own eyes. "Please leave all the dolls here."

Sobbing quietly, Dagmar lined up the dolls on the sofa. Then, she kissed each one. "Dear Jesus," she prayed quietly. "Please send me another doll." Without another glance back, she took her mother's hand and walked out of the room.

After Livia and the children had said farewell to their landladies, they boarded the streetcar taking them to the train station. The train bound for *Nordhausen* was nearly ready to depart.

Frank, with a rucksack on his back, sprinted ahead to reserve a compartment. The women grabbed their suitcases and hurried after him. Livia pushed Dagmar up the steps in front of her. Then, she and Lydia heaved their heavy suitcases aboard and climbed onto the train.

Almost immediately, the conductor shouted "All aboard!" The wheels started to clack along the rails.

A colorful fall landscape whizzed past, but the two women hardly noticed it. They sat stiffly opposite each other, each with a child beside her. While the youngsters bounced joyfully, the adults worried. Had anyone suspected the real reason for the trip? At the next stop, the women looked anxiously toward the platform. Were any policemen waiting to arrest them? They welcomed the darkness that finally descended upon the countryside.

Inside the compartment, Dagmar was seized by a fit of coughing. She had caught another cold a few days ago. Livia wished that she had some cough medicine to give her. Dagmar's coughing could spoil all their well-laid plans.

After several hours, the conductor yelled, "Nordhausen, next stop." Livia and Lydia gathered their baggage and peered into the night. When the train screeched to a stop, they prodded the children and descended onto the platform. They looked about in confusion. A white handkerchief waved from one corner. The women steered their brood toward it.

"We have come to claim the baggage bound for distant parts," a strange man announced.

"Everything is here, ready to go," Livia replied. She had rehearsed her lines well. Before long, the passengers and their goods were rolling away on a horse-drawn wagon. After about half an hour, the wagon turned sharply off the main road onto a dirt track. A few lights twinkled in the distance. Soon, dark, hulking shapes of houses became visible.

"Here we are." Their mysterious driver stopped the wagon and jumped down. He reached out to help the women and children descend. "I am Alfred Rauser. You will be staying at my house tonight." He ushered his guests toward the side entrance. His wife had been expecting them. She flung open the door and showered the latecomers in a flood of light.

"Welcome to our humble home. Come into the kitchen for a hot drink," she urged. "I think you need a little refreshment after such a long journey," Livia, Lydia and the children gratefully sipped the warm milk. They were even happier when their hostess led them to the bedroom. After their strenuous day, they fell into a deep, dreamless sleep.

Daylight filtered through the curtains when Livia awoke. For a moment, she could not remember where she was. Then, the reality of what lay ahead overwhelmed her. She looked fondly at the sleeping faces of her children. For their sakes, she was ready to face any danger.

In a few minutes, Lydia stirred. Suddenly, Dagmar was seized by a fit of coughing. Everyone was awake now.

"Sh—sh-sh, Dagmar." Livia lifted her daughter up. The child's face was red. She kept on coughing. "Hold her up for a while, Lydia." Livia slid out of bed and put on her housecoat. "I will ask our hostess for a little tea with lemon and honey."

"I hope that she can get over that cough before we make the border crossing" Lydia looked at her niece with concern. After Dagmar drank the hot tea, her cough eased. In a short time, everyone sat in the warm kitchen and ate crusty rolls spread with jam. Quietly, the adults discussed the plans for their dangerous venture.

"The conditions are favorable for this evening," said Herr Rauser. "The moon will be up for only one hour and it does not look like rain."

"We will put ourselves under your command," said Livia. "Only guide us safely to the West." She handed an envelope to the guide. It contained 200 Mark, the fee for guiding them.

"I just hope that your daughter will quit all that coughing," Herr Rauser continued. "She could easily give us all away."

"Don't worry," Dagmar suddenly piped up. "I have asked the Lord Jesus to help me to stop coughing." The adults looked at the child in amazement and said no more.

That day crawled by much too slowly. Their suitcases and rucksacks waited beside the door.

By the time evening arrived, Livia and Lydia squirmed at the edge of their seats. They drilled the children about obeying orders and keeping absolutely quiet. Later in the evening, Dagmar leaned against her mother and fell asleep. Just before midnight, Alfred Rauser put on his sturdy boots and dark jacket. He stared deeply at each of his charges. "It is time to go," he whispered and walked towards the door. "Stay close behind me." Livia shook her daughter awake. The guide took the little girl's hand and grabbed one suitcase. He stepped out into the blackness.

Another trek into the unknown had begun. Livia, Lydia and Frank followed close behind their guide. After a while, their eyes adjusted to the darkness and they could make out a faint path leading into the fields. What unforeseen dangers loomed ahead?

With cat-like tread, the others walked behind Alfred. Livia's blood pulsed wildly in her ears. She kept her eyes focused on Frank's rucksack, just ahead of her. Often, she had to switch her heavy suitcase from one hand to the other. Lydia walked right behind her, loaded down with a rucksack and a suitcase. She gladly risked her own life to help her loved ones.

After an hour of walking, the guide signaled a stop. Furtively, the wanderers huddled beneath a cluster of bushes. "We will rest here while the moon is up," whispered Alfred. Dagmar snuggled close to her mother. Frank crouched beside Aunt Lydia. Their guide leaned against a stone and kept a watchful eye. All at once, he nudged Livia and pointed upward. A light, brighter than the moon, streaked across the sky. Then, the searchlight scoured the land. The border guards were looking for escapees. The group under the bushes hardly dared to breathe. Distant barking of dogs shattered the stillness.

"Please, God," Livia whispered. "Don't let them catch our scent." The barking went on and on, but came no closer. At last, the sounds faded away. After some time, the lights also dimmed. The hidden ones began to breathe a little easier.

When all was dark again, their guide prodded them into action. Once more, they stumbled through fields, along tracks, usually meant for livestock. They were walking along a raised path, when suddenly, dark shapes rose from the ditch. Before anyone knew what was happening, the guide had dropped the suitcase, let go of Dagmar's hand and disappeared. The escapees froze to the spot. "This is it. We're caught," Livia gasped and clutched her bosom.

The dark shapes came closer.

After a tense moment, Lydia started to giggle nervously. "Look at their backpacks!" She pointed. "They are trying to escape, just like us." It was true. The other escapees had hidden in the ditch when they saw a strange group approaching. They came out when they realized that this was not the border police. What a fright each group had given the other! In a short time, the guide returned from his hiding place. The encounter had shaken everyone, but the trek must go on.

In their heightened state of mental alertness, the travelers became unaware of physical discomforts. Heavy suitcases and backpacks strained their shoulders and backs. They were soaked up to their hips after walking through wet fields. Bloodshot eyes bulged, peering into the darkness. They felt nothing. Only one thought propelled them forward – freedom.

After they had trudged for hours, they saw a light gray tinge in the eastern sky. Alfred stopped suddenly. They had reached the crucial crossing. He motioned for the others to wait while he went to investigate. On his stomach, Alfred slithered to a clump of bushes near the highway. A border guard, with a rifle slung over his shoulder patrolled this stretch. Alfred lay very still and listened to the guard's footsteps. He counted 64 steps from here to the end of the route and 89 steps returning to the other end.

When he was sure of the pattern, Alfred crept back to his companions. "Follow me on your hands and knees up to the bushes," he instructed in hushed tone. "I will listen to the guard's footsteps. When I say 'Go!' you must dash across. Don't stop. Don't look back. Are you ready?"

"Yes," answered Livia and Lydia in unison. The children nodded their heads. Cautiously, everyone crept to the roadside. Surely, the guard could hear their rapid breathing or the loud thumping of their hearts.

When the guard's back was almost at the farthest point, Alfred whispered, "Now, Go!" Livia grabbed Dagmar's hand and flung herself and the child up onto the pavement. She stood there, dazed, as in a nightmare. Dagmar pulled hard on her mother's hand. Immediately, energy surged into Livia and she dashed across. Right behind her came Lydia and Frank, and last of all, Alfred. They plunged into bushes on the other side. The border guard had turned around. His footsteps crunched closer and closer. Had he heard a noise? Would he stop to investigate? Under the bushes, the escapees strained to hear any change in the pattern of his steps. The guard marched past and kept on going.

They had to get away before he returned. Alfred motioned for his companions to creep towards distant trees. Even now, they dared not make a noise. They ducked under bushes and trees until they reached an open field. Alfred peered right and left. "Hurry across," he advised.

On the far side of the field, Livia ran into a barbed wire fence. "We must be very careful here," Alfred warned. "An electric current runs through the top wire. Always keep one foot on the ground, as I help you crawl between the wires." With his leather gloves, Alfred stretched the two middle wires apart. Liva went first. Sharp barbs snagged her coat, holding her back. Alfred loosened the cloth and Livia rolled into the grass on the other side. She turned onto her knees. Her hands reached out to catch first, Dagmar and then, Frank. Lydia squeezed through the hole next. Then, Alfred heaved their suitcases through the opening. Finally, he crawled through himself.

Quickly, they all stumbled toward a dirt road. There, Alfred set down the suitcase he had been carrying.

"We are now safely in the West," he announced. The women stared at him with open mouths. All at once, Livia threw her arms around his neck and started to weep.

"We are free! We are truly free!" she cried. "You brought us safely to the West." She hardly wanted to release Alfred. "Thank you for everything."

Lydia grabbed his hand and shook it. "May God reward you richly for helping us," she stammered. Frank reached out his hand and nodded his thanks. Dagmar flung her small arms around Alfred's knees and squeezed. At that moment, everyone realized that she had not coughed once during the night.

"Keep on walking along this road." Alfred pointed west. "After a while, you will arrive at a village where you can board a train bound for Hanover. I must leave right away, before daylight." With a quick wave, he disappeared into the shadows. Livia and Lydia picked up their suitcases and started walking. The children followed in their footsteps. Their hearts overflowed with gratitude. A new day was dawning.

CHAPTER 13

Heavily weighed down, the fugitives trudged into the small town just as the sun was rising. A long street stretched before them. Slowly, they plodded along. Where was the train station?

There, in the distance, loomed an arched roof. Only a few more steps, and they stumbled into the depot.

First, they had to know when the next train for Hanover was leaving. Lydia set down her suitcase, scanned the schedule and walked over to the ticket counter. The train was due within the hour. In the meantime, Livia searched inside her nearly empty wallet. Carefully, she counted out the required amount. The agent handed her the tickets. Clutching the precious stubs, Livia and Lydia collapsed onto the wooden benches. Fatigue overwhelmed them, but they dared not doze off. Dagmar and Frank leaned against them on either side.

Livia dug again in her handbag and brought out four apples that the border guide had given her the previous evening. How delicious they tasted!

In forty—five minutes, the train thundered into the station. Screeching brakes jolted Livia and Lydia out of their stupor. They prodded the children to follow them, as they dragged their suitcases onto the platform. Gathering their last strength, they heaved their luggage onto the landing of the nearest car and climbed up. They were thankful to find empty seats inside the compartment for themselves and the children. When the conductor came to punch their tickets Livia pressed a few coins into his hand. "Please wake us just before Hanover," she said.

The train whistle hooted, the engine started to hum and the conductor shouted and shut the door. The train pulled out, picking up speed as it went. Inside the compartment, eyes closed and heads bobbed. All tension disappeared into peaceful slumber. It seemed as if only minutes had passed when the conductor poked Livia. "Hanover in ten minutes," he said. She stretched and woke up the others. They had just gathered their baggage, when the train rolled into the huge terminal at Hanover.

After they had once again lugged out their suitcases, the women scanned the crowd for a familiar face. Gradually, the melee thinned out and they spied Eduard's thin form in the distance. He was waving his hat and pressing toward them. In a few minutes, he welcomed them with open arms. Dagmar embraced her father's knees, Lydia shook his hand, Livia gave him a brief hug, but Frank dodged aside. Then, they carried their suitcases and rucksacks outside and boarded the streetcar.

"How glad I am that you made it safely across the border!" Eduard exclaimed after everyone was settled.

"Yes, thank God!" Livia agreed. "I can hardly believe that we completed such harrowing escape successfully."

"For now," Eduard continued. "We will be staying at a refugee shelter. Many others have come to Hanover looking for a place to live."

"We have to live in a refugee camp?" Frank voiced his disgust.

"Be thankful for a place to stay, Frank," admonished his mother. "It probably will not be for long."

Lydia listened quietly. She planned to stay only one night and then, to travel on to *Montabaur* where she had some friends. The husband had been a fellow prisoner with Bruno. Lydia hoped to apply for resident status in that city. Once her husband, was released from prison camp, she did not want him to be back under Soviet control. If all went well, he could then come to Montabaur.

After a short ride, the streetcar clanged to a stop. "This is where we get off," Eduard announced. The group descended in front of a gray iron fence. On the gate hung a sign, 'Hanover Refugee Shelter.' The children squinted through the iron bars on the gate. A long building made of gray brick loomed ahead. Metal grates covered the narrow windows. A gray sky draped itself overhead.

"It looks like a jail," Frank blurted out.

"It is not so bad." His father tried to reassure the others. He pushed open the gate and steered them into the yard. Between strips of hard—packed earth, the walk led up two steps to a gray wooden door. Eduard rang the bell. The door creaked open a slit and two eyes and a nose peered out. Then, a fleshy hand thrust the groaning door completely open. Framed in the opening, stood a stout woman.

"*Ach*, Herr Falk!" She made a wry face. "You are back with your family. Well, don't just stand there. Come on in." The bewildered clan stumbled over the threshold, into the dimly lit hallway. "Your quarters will be over there." The matron pointed to a doorway on the left side. "You will have to share the room with two other families. It is the best I can do for you. All meals are taken in the dining room at the far end. You will find washrooms down the hall to your right." With her hip, the matron pushed open the door to the designated bedroom.

"Here you are," she grumbled. "Make yourselves at home, but don't disturb your neighbors." Sighing loudly, she turned and left the room.

The Falk family looked around their new home in dismay. Gray blankets sagged from ropes strung across the room, near the ceiling. They divided the place into three sections. The newcomers flocked toward the open curtains in the far, left—hand corner. Two sets of bunk beds leaned against the outer wall. Each bed was adorned with a rolled—up, gray blanket and a thin pillow. A scratched dresser and a well—worn chair stood under a bare window. The small, central space of the enclosure was barely covered by a threadbare piece of carpet.

Wearily, Livia and Lydia plopped down on the nearest bed. Eduard sank into the chair, while the children climbed up onto a top bunk. "I guess we should be thankful," Livia finally whispered. "At least, we have a roof over our heads." But then, she covered her face and started to weep. They had endured so much to come to this!

Awkwardly, Eduard tried to comfort her. "We will soon find something better," he soothed. "God will provide for us."

His frequently used cliché angered his wife. She jumped up, hands on her hips and glared at him. "That may be true." Livia's dark eyes blazed. "But nothing will get better if you just sit around. God helps those who help themselves."

Beside her, the curtain suddenly stirred. "Be quiet!" shouted a muffled voice behind it. "I am trying to sleep."

Eduard hung his head. Livia slumped down again. Lydia put her arm around her sister. With big eyes, Frank and Dagmar gazed down from their lofty perch.

"Tomorrow I am going to see the camp director." Livia choked back her tears. "I will see to it that we get out of here as soon as possible."

The next morning, Livia, Eduard and the children said a sorrowful good bye to dear Aunt Lydia. Words could not express their gratitude for all that she had done. Lydia promised to write when she got to her destination.

After her sister had left, Livia knocked on the office of the camp
director. Behind the desk, sat a middle-aged man, wearing horn—
rimmed glasses. He raised his head and pointed to a chair. "Do be
seated," he said. "Please state your name and your concern?"

"I am *Frau* Falk, the wife of Eduard," replied Livia. "We have two
children, a thirteen—year- old son, Frank and a six—year-old
daughter, Dagmar. Recently, we escaped from Communist East
Germany. Now, we need to find proper housing."

"*Liebe Frau* Falk," the man said with a faint smile. "I would like to
help you, but we have so many cases just like yours."

"Please tell me what to do." Livia's big brown eyes looked pleadingly
at him. "We must get out of here as soon as possible. My nerves are
on the breaking point."

"Here are some papers for you to fill out." The director shoved a
bundle across the desk. "Your case will be evaluated. As soon as a
place becomes available, I will notify you. In the meantime, try to
be content here."

Livia rose from her seat. "*Vielen Dank, mein Herr.*" She bowed
slightly and flashed him a dazzling smile.

"What a charming lady!" the director said to himself as she shut the
door. "I will do what I can to help her."

After the paperwork was completed, Livia tried hard to look on the
bright side. She made a special effort to get along with the other
families who shared the room. Also, she encouraged Eduard to write
to the headquarters of their denomination. Surely, there was some
position he could fill in West Germany. Next, she registered the
children at school. Filling their days with worthwhile activities was
very important. At the time, Livia never realized that distant forces
were moving things in her favor.

The plight of the displaced persons, who flooded Germany, was broadcast to the United States and Canada. Soon, sympathetic organizations started sending financial and physical aid to the war-ravaged country. One day, Livia and Eduard received a notice that a parcel was waiting for them at the post office. The whole family took the long walk to pick it up. Each one wanted a turn to carry this treasure.

Back at their curtained bedroom, the family could hardly wait to open the parcel. They placed it on the dresser and crowded around. Livia carefully untied the string. She handed it to Frank who rolled it up into a ball. It would work so well for flying a homemade kite. Livia was picking away on the stitching in the canvas cover. Gradually, the cloth fell away, revealing a cardboard box. Dagmar bounced with excitement as her mother opened the flaps Out tumbled a can of cocoa and a sack of sugar. "Ah—," sighed the children. Then, Livia took out a rectangular box. 'Lard' was printed on its side. She set it on the dresser beside the first two items. Next, she brought out another round can. 'Plum Pudding' the label said.

"I wonder what that is?" Eduard asked. The children strained their necks to see the next thing. It was a pound of coffee.

"Now, that will be a useful item to barter for other goods," commented Livia. She placed it on the crowded dresser. The bottom of the parcel held soft, lumpy things. Livia pulled out something wrapped in a little blanket. On a hunch, she handed it to Dagmar. "I think this might be for you," the mother guessed. Dagmar unrolled the blanket. Enfolded in the middle, lay a rag doll. It had red yarn hair, curved arms and legs and wore colorful clothes.

"Oh!" gasped Dagmar. "A doll for me! I asked God for another doll when I had to leave those dolls behind in Jena." She hugged the rag doll to her chest and danced around in a circle.

"That thing looks like a frog." Frank wrinkled his nose. "Yes, 'Froggie' will be a good name for your doll, Dagmar." She paid no attention to her brother's teasing. She only knew that God had answered her prayer.

Meanwhile, Livia had pulled a few items of clothing out of the box. She held them up one by one. With a few alterations, they could be made to fit her sprouting children. At last, the box was empty. It was repacked carefully, and put under the bed. Joyfully, the Falk family walked to the kitchen. They asked permission to celebrate by making some cocoa.

After receiving that parcel, Livia felt greatly encouraged. God had not forsaken them. Her request for housing would be granted also. She was happy that Eduard had found temporary employment. Together with another minister, he visited other refugee camps in a delivery van. They distributed used clothing and canned foods that had been sent from overseas. In return, Eduard could choose things for his own family. Livia used whatever they could do without to barter for items that her family needed. What a blessing these parcels were!

After several weeks in the refugee camp, Livia was summoned to the director's office. "It is a pleasure to meet again," he said. "I have good news for you. We have found a place for you and your family. It is a house on the outskirts of Hanover. Please be ready to leave here in three days. We will have a driver ready to take you to your new home."

Livia hugged herself as she hurried back to their bedroom. She could hardly wait until the children came home from school. What wonderful news!

CHAPTER 14

Filled with anticipation, the Falk family hurried from the refugee home into the old Volkswagen. They barely had room to crowd into the two-door 'beetle' with all their baggage. When everyone was jammed in, the driver started the engine and they were off.

"Roll down the window, please," Frank whined from the back seat. "I am nearly suffocating."

"Be still, please," his mother warned, but she was grateful when fresh air swept over them. With Dagmar on her knees, she was squeezed tightly against a large suitcase.

The VW. wound its way through the busy streets of Hanover towards the outskirts on the north end of the city. "This area is called *Holzwiesen*," The driver informed his passengers. "We are nearing your destination." In a few minutes, he stopped on a rutted track and pointed. "There is your new home," he said and opened his door.

Eduard almost fell out of the door on the passenger side. Livia and the children climbed awkwardly from the back seat, dragging suitcases out behind them. The driver removed their bundled—up bedding out of the trunk. Then he tipped his hat, jumped back into the car and raced away, spinning clumps of mud as he went.

The Falk family gaped at the sight before them – a flat-roofed hovel fronted by a muddy yard. Near one side, stood a dilapidated chicken coop. A few white hens pecked at the sparse grass that surrounded it. A pathway of broken stones led to the front door of the house.

Tentatively, they stepped along the broken walkway. Eduard knocked on the door. The rest of the family hugged their baggage, trying to keep it out of the mud. Slowly, the door creaked open. A muscular man, with unshaved chin, squinted at them. "Who are you?" he demanded brusquely.

"We are the Falk family." Eduard swept his hand over the group. "We have been sent here by the refugee committee. I believe you have accommodation for us."

"Oh, yes." The man scratched his greasy head. "I did not expect you so soon. Come on in and I will show you the rooms." He led them through a narrow hallway into a large, low- ceiling room. "This will be your kitchen/sitting room." The owner swept his hand around the area. "There are two bedrooms just down that hall. The outhouse is in the back."

Livia stood rooted to the spot, taking in the dismal surroundings. "Oh!" she gasped. The others just stared. Their new landlord was already leaving. "Make yourselves comfortable. My name is Schwartz," he said over his shoulder.

As soon as the door had closed, Livia fell onto a rickety kitchen chair. "Before we can do anything else," she moaned. " We have to start cleaning. Thank goodness, the refugee board paid the first month's rent for this dump."

Eduard and the children looked crestfallen. "Well, don't just stand there," Livia exclaimed and jumped up. She took off her coat, rummaged in her suitcase for a coverall apron and then, investigated the little storeroom off the kitchen. Soon, she emerged with a tin pail, a few rags and a bar of yellow soap. "Take off your coats and get to work," she commanded.

She handed rags to Frank and Dagmar. "There is an old broom in the corner by the door, Eddek." She pointed in that direction. "You can start by sweeping the floors inside the house, and then, that little walk outside."

In a short time, everyone was working. Clouds of dust flew in front of Eduard's broom. Frank and Dagmar scrubbed the kitchen table and chairs with soapy water. Livia attacked the grime on the kitchen stove. She pulled out the bottom drawer, filled to overflowing with ashes. She took them outside and dumped them on a pile behind the outhouse. She called to Eduard to help her bring in kindling and logs from the woodpile. When the kitchen was clean, she started a fire in the stove.

Rumbling stomachs announced lunchtime. What could the mother make quickly? She had spotted a bag of potatoes and a sack of flour in the storeroom. After more searching, she found a chipped enamel bowl, a metal grater and a cast iron frying pan. "Come and help me peel and grate potatoes, Dagmar," her mother called. "We will make potato pancakes for lunch. Frank, please run out into the yard, where those hens were sitting. See if you can find an egg or two for our pancakes."

After a little while, Livia's flushed face bent over the hot frying pan. She dropped batter into the sizzling lard. "Look inside that cardboard box, Dagmar." Livia pointed with her spoon.

"Take out a jar of that syrup Aunt Lydia gave us." The mouthwatering aroma of potato pancakes filled the air. The children had already set the table, and waited impatiently for their food. Soon, everyone was sitting down, munching on the pancakes.

"Potato pancakes are my favorite food," Eduard commented. The children were too busy smacking their lips to say anything.

After lunch, everyone wanted to rest, but too much work still had to be done. While Frank and Dagmar washed and dried the dishes, Livia covered the beds with clean sheets and unpacked her suitcases. She filled their empty shells with extra linens and shoved the suitcases under the bed. Meanwhile, the children unpacked their clothing into their dresser drawers. Dagmar proudly set her 'Froggie' on top of her pillow. This room was beginning to look better.

The afternoon had passed so quickly, that Livia hardly had time to think about supper. For lack of other supplies, she dragged out the sacks of potatoes and flour again. She had gathered a few wild onion shoots on her way back from the outhouse. Now, she had the ingredients for making a potato soup. After the family had filled up on soup and crusty, rye bread, they relaxed on the old couch near the stove. " This place seems more like home after all our work." Livia yawned and stretched. Every muscle in her body ached. Eduard read a passage from the Bible and the family said their prayers. Even though it was still early, they tumbled into bed.

The Falk family had moved into their new home on a dry day, but spring rains started to fall shortly afterwards. They soon discovered that the flat roof of the house was more like a sieve. Water droplets collected on the ceiling and dropped down. Livia scurried around in the storeroom, gathering empty containers. One pail caught the rivulets in the hallway. Another bucket caught the drops in a corner of the kitchen. A steady drip fell from the ceiling over the end of Dagmar's bed. The room was too small to move the bed. In desperation, Livia hauled out the galvanized washtub and placed it under the leak. Dagmar shuddered every time her bare toes touched the cold metal at night. "Curl your self up, Dagmar," advised her mother. "And put on a pair of socks so you won't feel the cold so much."

Day after day the leaden skies wept millions of tears. Livia felt like weeping too. Clothing and bedding became damp and musty. Every morning, Eduard groaned when he got up. "All my bones are aching," he complained. The only warm, dry place was close to the kitchen stove. Livia asked the landlord to fix the roof. He just shrugged his shoulders, frowned and turned his back.

After two weeks, the sun finally broke through the clouds. The whole family hurried outside to bask in its rays. That morning, Frank and Dagmar bolted away to school, like young colts.

After Eduard had left on one of his missions, Livia dragged the bedding to air out on the clothesline. She hardly wanted to go back inside.

As she was gazing down the track, a strange vehicle pulled in off the road. A mottled nag pulled a brightly—painted wagon right up to where she stood. From the driver's seat, a dark- skinned fellow, dressed in patched britches and an open-necked shirt, jumped down. "Good morning," he said. "Do you have any leaky pots and pans or broken furniture in need of repair?"

Livia was surprised to see a Gypsy in her yard. "Yes, I do have some broken things," she answered. "But I cannot afford to pay you." She turned to go back into the house.

"Wait, please," the man called out. "Perhaps, we can arrange a trade." His dark eyes gleamed as he spoke.

"I am afraid that I have very little of any value," Livia said, but then she turned back to him. "But, I am very skilled at sewing," she added, looking at his ragged clothes.

"These clothes are good enough for me." The Gypsy ran his dirty hands down his pant legs.

"But, my wife and daughters like to get dressed up. I will return tomorrow and we can make a bargain."

When the wagon had left, Livia had second thoughts. What had she gotten herself into? From all reports, Gypsies were not to be trusted.

As he had promised, the man returned the following day, carrying bundles of colorful cloth.

"My two daughters want new dresses," he explained and handed the bundles to Livia. "One girl is about the same age as your daughter." The Gypsy pointed at Dagmar who was hiding behind her mother. "The other girl is two years older." He held out a scrap of brown paper. "I wrote down their measurements for you."

Livia was amazed that he knew enough to take proper measurements. "What kind of dresses do your girls want?" she asked. The man dug in his pocket again, pulled out a tightly folded paper and handed it to Livia. She unfolded it to find an old magazine illustration of a Spanish dancer dressed in a costume of tiered ruffles. "This work will take me at least two weeks," Livia told the man.

"That is quite satisfactory." The Gypsy nodded his dark head. "Now, if you can show me what needs repair, I will start my work." He waited outside while Livia searched inside the kitchen. Then, he took the leaky pots and broken chairs to his wagon. While Livia spread the fabrics out on the kitchen table, she could hear him hammering away.

By the third day, all the broken items had been repaired, but Livia's work had only begun. She did not own a sewing machine and had to stitch everything by hand. Every evening, she worked until her eyes were sore. Gradually, beautiful dresses took shape under her skillful fingers. She added little velvet bows to the colorful ruffles at the shoulders. Finally, she called Dagmar to try on the smaller dress. The child was delighted to be a model. She twirled around and around in front of the wardrobe mirror. The dress fit her perfectly. "I wish I could have a dress like that," Dagmar sighed.

"I am sorry, *Liebling*," Livia said, pulling the dress off over Dagmar's head. "This dress belongs to the Gypsy's daughter."

When the man came the following day to pick up the dresses, he brought an extra payment.

"Thank you for doing such beautiful work," he exclaimed. "My girls will be delighted." He handed Livia a burlap sack. As soon as he had left, she pulled open the drawstring. Inside were two eviscerated rabbits. What a wonderful feast they would make! The skins could be tanned and made into a muff for Dagmar. Livia hugged her daughter and they danced around for joy.

After the rabbit meat was eaten, the family was once more forced to subsist on a meager fare.

Eduard earned a little money from offerings. It had to be stretched to pay their rent and buy staple foods. Livia bartered used clothing and cans of coffee from parcels for other necessities. When the children were in school, she scoured the countryside for edible plants. Sometimes, she came home with a pail full of green sorrel for soup, wild mushrooms to fry, or tasty berries for dessert. "Be thankful for what God has provided," she admonished when Dagmar turned up her nose at the sorrel soup. Yet, Livia also longed for a more abundant life.

When Eduard came back from his next mission trip, he brought a pair of young rabbits with him. "When they get a little older, they will have babies," he said excitedly. "Then we can have rabbit meat for dinner." For once, Eduard was enthusiastic and started looking for odd pieces of wood to build cages for the rabbits. Frank helped his father nail them together, while Dagmar gathered dandelion leaves and grass to feed the rabbits. In time, the parents produced five young ones. In a few weeks, a plump rabbit had to be killed. Dagmar hid in her room and cried during the process. Yet, she enjoyed the delicious rabbit stew that her mother cooked. As the rabbits multiplied rapidly, the Falk family continued to feast frequently on their meat.

One Sunday, when the rest of the family went to church, Frank stayed home alone. He was lost in a book, when he heard loud banging on the other side of the bedroom wall. What was the landlord doing over there? The crashing grew louder. Bits of mortar and bricks began to fall. The banging sounded closer. Suddenly, a shower of bricks tumbled into Franks's bedroom. A hole now gaped near the top of the wall. Framed in the opening, appeared the twisted face of the landlord. His bloodshot eyes rolled wildly. "Get out of here, you rotten refugee!" he shouted. A beer bottle whizzed past Frank's head.

The boy dropped his book and dashed from the room. He ran out of the house, down the track and hid in the bushes beyond. He had just crouched down, when the landlord staggered out of the house. He was waving an ax and yelling. "Come out, you good-for-nothing," he raged. "I'll teach you a lesson." The man tottered around in circles and suddenly, dropped to the ground. He lay there, like a dead man. Frank shivered behind the bushes. He dared not stir.

At long last, Frank saw his parents and his sister coming down the road. Quietly, he sneaked out of his hiding place and ran to warn them. "Old man Schwartz is lying in the yard, like a dead man," Frank panted. "He knocked down part of the bedroom wall and wanted to kill me."

The family made a huge detour around the drunk. Once inside their entrance, they locked the door. They stood motionless in their kitchen, listening for footsteps. When Livia peeked out into the yard, the landlord still lay there, motionless. "We have to get out of this place as soon as possible." Livia shook all over. "Who knows what he might do next time he gets drunk?"

After that frightening episode, Eduard and Livia were desperate to find better housing. The waiting list at the city offices was far too long. In the midst of their dilemma, Eduard heard from an old friend, with whom he had attended seminary in Poland. Herr Koenig and his family were planning to emigrate from Germany to Canada next month. Their two—bedroom suite, in a good apartment block, would soon be empty. They suggested a risky venture.

On the appointed day, people were coming and going. While the Koenig family moved out, the Falk family moved in. By evening, the newcomers had settled in and deposited their month's rent. How they prayed that the new landlord would not evict them! Livia took her children aside. "When you meet Herr Weiss, you must be very polite," she instructed.

"Frank, doff your cap when you greet him. Dagmar, curtsy and smile at him. Surely, he will not put such charming children out on the street." Miraculously, the scheme worked.

Although their residence was much better, Eduard's health continued to deteriorate. He suffered from bouts of arthritis and lung problems. Luckily, the West German State provided free medical care for its citizens. The doctor sent Eduard to a spa at *Bad Sachsa*, in the Alps. For six weeks, the patient underwent treatments of mineral baths, physical exercises and plenty of sunshine.

When Eduard returned home, tanned and fit, Livia was amazed. He looked better than the day she had married him. Eduard was full of vigor and amorous feelings. Nine months later, another daughter, Margot was born.

By this time, Eduard's brief spurt of health had already passed. Now, he had another child to feed and clothe. The pennies that dribbled in from offerings were not nearly enough.

Meanwhile, Livia's days were filled with work and worry. Her sisters still sent gifts of food to help out. When would things get better?

During these difficult times, Canadian Christian groups tried to help their brothers and sisters in Germany. Some visitors traveled overseas to see the situation for themselves. Eduard and Livia often entertained these foreign 'angels'. One lady, Mrs. Tzelody, became a special friend. She was fluent in German, Polish as well as English. She encouraged Eduard and the family to apply for emigration to Canada.

After all the paperwork had been completed, the Falk family waited anxiously. They searched through the atlas for Canada. What a huge country it was, compared to Germany!

To Dagmar, the name Canada sounded like 'Caanan' in the Bible, the land flowing with milk and honey. Canada must be a wonderful place!

At last, the Falk family was summoned to *Bremerhaven*. Each member of the family had to pass a physical examination. After the train ride, they arrived at the 'Bremer Overseas Home'. There, they stayed in one of the barracks. On the next day, each family member had to appear before a row of doctors. Dagmar was thoroughly embarrassed when she had to strip and parade stark naked in front of them. After the ordeal, the family waited anxiously. A doctor entered the waiting room and handed a folder to Eduard. "I am very sorry," he said.

"You are not allowed to emigrate because of your poor physical condition. The rest of your family passed the test."

CHAPTER 15

How disappointed the Falk family was after they returned to Hanover! They had failed the test, but Livia's sister, Gerda had been approved for emigration to Canada. After her escape from East Germany, she had applied almost immediately, to go to Canada. Strong, healthy workers like Gerda were needed in the new world. She left Bremerhaven in the spring of 1952 on the ship, *Beaverbrae*. Soon after her arrival in Winnipeg, Manitoba, she wrote to her relatives.

'Dear Livia, Eduard and children,

After a long ocean voyage, I landed in Quebec City. From there, I traveled by train, across this vast country, to Winnipeg. The only job I could find, at first, was in the sugar beet fields south of the city. The strenuous physical labor nearly wore me out. When the harvest was over, I searched in Winnipeg for another job. Now, I am working in a sewing factory.

The Christian group here has made me feel welcome. The church alliance is willing to prepay the passage for you to come over. After I have lived here for one year, I will be able to sponsor you. In the meantime, Eduard should apply for a ministerial position in Winnipeg. I hope and pray that these plans will work out.

With all my love, Gerda.'

Once more, the Falk family renewed their hopes of going to Canada. This time, Eduard only needed a certificate of health from his personal doctor. Because he was feeling better, Eduard squeaked through the test. The rest of the family passed easily. Livia filled out the required papers and sent them away. Would their application meet the approval of the Canadian government? Every day, Livia sifted through their mail for a reply. The waiting seemed endless.

At last, the crucial letter arrived. Livia hid it in her apron pocket and hurried into her kitchen. She sank onto a chair and tore open the envelope with shaking hands. Quickly, she scanned the lines. Their application had been approved. Passage for the family was booked on the S.S. Ryndam, sailing out of Rotterdam, Holland, on Jan.18, 1953. Livia gasped. Could this really be true? They only had two months to get ready.

Before the departure, Livia planned to have a family Christmas celebration. Aunt Lydia and Uncle Bruno traveled to Hanover for the special occasion. Uncle Bruno looked so much healthier one year after his release from prison camp. Little Margot was now a toddler and babbled baby language to her adoring aunt and uncle. She hugged the teddy bear that they had brought for her. Even though the Christmas tree looked scrawny and the gifts were few, the relatives treasured their time together. Who knew if or when they would see each other again?

After Christmas, preparations for leaving Germany began in earnest. Livia ordered two large wooden crates for their linens, dishes and precious keepsakes. Their clothing would be packed into two huge suitcases. Besides the hand luggage, they needed a suitable container for a vital item. Livia found a small cardboard box for Margot's potty. The inscription on the outside said "Knorr's Pea Sausage." Dagmar was designated to carry this interesting box, tied up with string.

Then, Livia turned her attention to finding warm clothing for the ocean voyage. She dug through piles of donated, vintage-style garments. She was pleased to find a dark wool suit, matching three-quarter length coat and sturdy shoes for herself. Eduard would wear his suit, a black wool overcoat and a hat. Livia had problems finding anything for the fashion- conscious teen-ager, Frank. He had to make his own choice. Dagmar was to wear a brown rabbit fur jacket over her green winter dress and a yellow cap that Livia had knit. Margot's outfit had been sent earlier from Sweden. It consisted of a hand-knit blue coat, rompers and matching ruffled hat. Livia sorted the clothing into piles and sighed. She hoped that her family would be warm enough.

On the Sunday before the departure, the Slavic refugees held a farewell service for Brother Falk and his family. A large group gathered in the hall. One after another, the Slavic brothers spoke at length. In the back rows, mothers nursed their babies, while the service went on for hours. At last, the Falk family was called to the front. The congregation joined hands and sang "God Be With You, Till We Meet Again." Afterwards, the family was showered with hugs and kisses. Livia sighed with relief when it was finally over.

Hurried activities were carried out during the last few days in Hanover. All outstanding bills had to be paid. Livia checked again and again, to make sure that their passports and important documents were in order. She cleaned their suite for the next occupants. The people, who had bought their few pieces of furniture, came to pick up their purchases. On the last night, the Falk family slept on their feather beds, spread out on the floor.

Emotions ran high and tempers grew short the following morning. "Come and help me roll up these feather beds, Eddek," Livia called, in vain. Eduard stumbled around looking for his shoes, his glasses and his hat. In the corner, Margot wailed for her food. Dagmar picked up her little sister and tried to comfort her. "Give her small pieces of the banana that is in my handbag," suggested Livia. Frank, with his camera slung around his neck, stood near the door, impatiently tapping his foot. By the time Eduard had found his belongings, Livia had bundled up the bedding and wrapped everything securely in canvas. "Just wait out in the hall, Eduard." She glared at him. "You are useless around here anyway."

"Don't talk to me like that!" Eduard yelled back at her. Just then, a van pulled up to the curb.

The vehicle, in which Eduard had traveled to deliver goods to refugee camps, would take his family to the train station. "Grab your things and let's go," Livia shouted. Eduard staggered outside with one suitcase.

Behind him, came Frank dragging another one. They stowed the luggage and climbed into the back of the vehicle. The van driver and a companion carried out the wooden crates and the bedding bundle. Livia clutched her handbag and carried Margot. She chased Dagmar ahead of her into the middle seat of the van. The driver and his companion jumped into the front. The engine roared and the van sped down the street.

At the train station, the Falk family formed the tail of a long line snaking toward the ticket counter. Luckily, their friends stayed close by to help out. At last, tickets were in hand and tags had been fixed onto the baggage. Once their cargo had been loaded, the family settled down in a compartment. As the train chugged out of the station, they waved goodbye to their companions.

The frantic scurry of the morning had left everyone ravenous. Livia pulled out a sack of sandwiches and two thermos bottles from her bag. These supplies would have to last for the train ride. The nourishment soothed both hunger and tension. As the train rushed along, both parents and the baby fell asleep. Frank and Dagmar were too excited to sleep. They peered out at the flat countryside that sped past them.

Although their baggage had been properly labeled, Livia wanted to make sure that it would be transferred to the ship. A porter, who was loading luggage onto a cart, nodded his head. He would take care of everything.

Propelled along by the milling crowd behind them, the Falk family struggled toward the *Wilhelminakade*, where their ship was docked. There, far above the tallest buildings near the harbor, loomed the gray hull of the S. S. Ryndam. They craned their necks, but could not see the top of it. Livia steered her brood toward the gangway. Eduard straggled along behind them. Hundreds of people were already streaming up the plank. A ship's officer checked their identification papers and waved them on.

Amid the surge of bodies, they climbed up the narrow passage to the side deck of the ship.

They gripped the railing and stared down at the crowded dock far below. A huge crane hoisted boxes and bundles from a pile, over their heads and into a hatch aboard the ship. A few latecomers scrambled up the gangplank just moments before it was pulled in. All around, shouts in many languages resounded. Suddenly, a blast from the foghorn nearly lifted the passengers off their feet. Two more loud blasts followed. The engines roared as the huge ship started to pull away from the dock. Handkerchiefs fluttered and arms waved in the air. Gradually, the figures on shore grew smaller and smaller.

"Good bye, Germany," exclaimed Livia. Teardrops glistened in her eyes. "Farewell to our dear ones who remain on your shores." She turned abruptly to face the open sea. What unknown adventures lay before them?

The winter sun was setting over the sea when the Falk family made their way down to their cabin. The door opened to reveal a snug place. Double bunk beds lined the two sidewalls. A baby crib stood near a dresser under the porthole. Beside it, a sink hung from the wall. This room would be their home for the next seven days. Public toilets were located a few steps down the hall.

After they had removed their overcoats and used the washrooms, they climbed up the stairs to the dining room. When was the last time they had eaten? Quickly, they found their seats at a long table. It was presided over by a Dutch steward in an immaculate, white uniform.

Livia's eyes widened as she tried to decipher the strange foods on the menu. Luckily, the steward also spoke German. He described each of the dishes and helped them make a selection. Soon, heaping platefuls, swirling with tantalizing aromas, appeared. Never before, had anyone tasted such delicious foods. Dagmar watched in delight as the steward carved fruit into fascinating shapes. She closed her eyes and wondered if she was in heaven.

On the following day, the youngsters could hardly wait to see the rest of the ship. Frank was off right after breakfast, exploring every nook and cranny. Eduard opted to relax on a deck chair, while his wife and daughters went to investigate the ship. They wandered along the Promenade Deck to the Palm Court. Inside, under a glass dome, grew luxurious palms and other tropical plants. Padded wicker chairs and lounges, grouped around small tables, invited passengers to relax. Here, they could sip afternoon tea or slurp a cold drink. Livia hated to leave this beautiful place, but Dagmar pulled on her arms. She wanted to see the playroom.

This large, bright room became Dagmar's favorite place. She found an abundance of toys and games. A wall shelf held a variety of books. The supervisor of the playroom welcomed the childen personally. "You may leave your daughters here," she said to Livia in Dutch-accented German. "They will be safe and happy until you come to get them." Dagmar wasted no time and ran straight to a corner full of dolls. Livia stayed with Margot for a while, before going back to the cabin.

"Take care of your sister," she said to Dagmar. "I will be back in an hour to check on you,"

The first days passed rapidly. After the S.S.Ryndam had made a brief stop at LeHavre, France, she steamed into the English Channel. None of the winter storms, which usually swept this section, disturbed the waters. Only small waves lapped against the ship's hull.

Livia, Dagmar and Margot stood on the aft deck, surveying the endless expanse of the sea. Screeching gulls followed the wake of the propellers. A few clouds floated high overhead.

Mild weather accompanied the ship all the way to Southampton, England. After she had taken on more passengers, the Rhyndam nosed out into the mighty Atlantic Ocean.

On the fourth day of the voyage, Livia and her daughters sat at their usual spot on the aft deck. They watched in amazement as the ship's stern rose high into the sky. Then, it plunged down into the churning water. "Look Mommy," cried Dagmar. "Our ship is sailing into the air!" She jumped to the railing. In a moment, the stern dived and Dagmar faced a wall of water. Suddenly, her stomach heaved and her breakfast flew out to feed the fish. Livia grabbed her seasick daughter. Slowly, she led her back to the cabin and called the steward.

Dagmar was too ill to take either the tea or crackers. By the end of that day, the other family members, except for Livia and Margot were also sick. Livia chewed on dry crackers and fought against nausea. She would not miss out on the delicious meals in the dining room.

As the ship fought its way westward, stronger winds gusted and the waves grew mountainous. In the cabin, Margot's crib slid from one end to the other until a steward secured it firmly with a chain. Livia hid their alarm clock in a drawer after it flew off the dresser and skidded across the floor. When anyone needed to use the washroom, he grasped the ropes along the hallway. Then, he had to grip a sling while sitting on the toilet. The ship creaked, groaned and tossed in the merciless storm.

On the fifth day, the winds had increased to gale force. That morning, a steward knocked on the cabin door. "Please appear on the Boat Deck in half an hour," he said to Livia. "We will outfit you with life preservers and conduct a drill." Livia gasped as she shut the door. Thoughts of the ill-fated Titanic raced through her mind.

"You must all get up," she ordered. "No matter how ill you feel you must appear on deck."

In a short time, pale-faced passengers crowded onto the heaving Boat Deck. An officer, with a megaphone, directed them to their appointed stations. Sailors distributed life jackets and helped fit them on. Eduard, Livia and the children struggled into their bulky life vests. The officer nearby pointed to the lifeboat suspended above their heads. "In case of an emergency, you will hear the ship's siren. Come to this station as soon as possible," he explained. " I will then direct you into this lifeboat. Let us hope and pray we will not have to use it." Everyone bowed their heads and nodded.

Neptune continued to take out his wrath on the North Atlantic. On the sixth day, the ship still tossed violently. No one dared to be out on deck, now. The Falk family huddled inside the cabin. Frank had overcome his symptoms and wanted to escape from all the seasickness. He hung on to the safety ropes until he found the movie theater. Amid the excitement of a Western, he forgot about the dangers all around.

Far below, the occupants of the cabin thought the end was near. Were they like Jonah who caused a storm by disobeying God? Their thoughts churned like the angry sea. "We need to pray and repent of all our sins," Eduard proclaimed solemnly. Even though Livia had always been confident of God's love, she too was sucked into a vortex of fear. With earnest tears, each one pleaded for God's mercy. Exhausted, they collapsed onto their bunks. Only Frank entered the cabin jauntily after everyone was asleep.

A pink sunrise streaked the sky the next morning. The rays rippled over serene waters to the Ryndam. An unearthly stillness had replaced the howling winds. On the last day of the voyage, storm-weary travelers crawled from their bunks. The floor rocked gently beneath their feet. Like the rest, the Falk family streamed onto the deck and gulped in the fresh air.

Soon, they felt huger pangs. How tasty their breakfast was after a long fast!

Soon, everyone appeared back on deck. Their eyes strained across the sea toward the west. Today, they would land in Canada. Still, there was nothing but the endless expanse of water. Livia and the children peered again into the distance. A darker line shimmered on the horizon. "Land Ho!" shouted a sailor. Crowds of people pushed towards the railing.

The dark shadow grew closer and closer until outline of a coast became distinct. A small tug chugged across the waves toward the Ryndam. She guided the vessel into Halifax harbor.

Buildings emerged from the swirling fog. The large ship edged herself in beside Pier 21. With a shudder the engines died out. The Falk family gripped tightly onto the deck railing.

"Canada, land of our hopes and dreams," Livia said, swallowing the lump in her throat. "God has brought us this far on our trek into the unknown. He will be our guide in the future. I wonder what adventures lie before us in this new country?"

Three beautiful sisters
Livia, Gerda, Lydia

Romances without a future
Gerda and her fiance, Hermann
Sergei and Livia

Livia's Last Christmas

Reunion of the three sisters
Lydia, Livia and Gerda

Eduard Falk's Family
Edmund, Eduard, Martha, Otto, Michael, Helen

Emma Dust holding Livia in 1912

Wedding of Art & Dagmar Wirch
Left: Eduard & Livia Falk,
Right: Olga and Albert Wirch

Falk Family in 1942
Livia, Dagmar, Frank, Eduard

Livia and Dagmar at sea.

October 6, 1934
Wedding of Livia and Eduard

The Dust Family in 1924
Gerda, Emma, Lydia, Livia, Anton

1970 – Livia with grandchildren—Cameron, Howard, Ramona

Dagmar 's First Day of School

Falk Family in 1949 – Dagmar, Livia, Frank, Eduard

Falk Family in 1952 – Livia with Margot, Frank, Eduard, Dagmar

PART II

OF LIVIA'S LEGACY
QUEST FOR FULLFILLMENT,

CHAPTER 1

A long, covered gangplank stretched from the ship to a drab, two-story brick building and was swallowed up inside. Livia cast uncertain glances at Pier 21, the Gateway to Canada. From the ravages of war and harrowing experiences of the past, she and her family had come to this unpretentious place. What did the future hold for them in Canada? She was jarred out of her reverie by the multitude pushing from behind. Still swaying on their sea legs, the Falk family was propelled into the cavernous reception hall. Livia stared at the stark walls, adorned by a Union Jack and a variety of flags. All around, voices echoed, babbling in many languages. Where should they go in all this confusion?

Suddenly, a man in uniform grabbed Eduard's arm. "Please follow me," he said and herded them into a long line. Livia craned her neck to see where the queue ended. In the distance hung a sign, "Medical Inspection." When they finally reached the desk, Margot felt like a heavy sack in Livia's arms. The doctor, holding a tongue depressor, turned to Livia first.

"Say ahh," he commanded. Obediently, Livia opened her mouth. Then, the doctor shone a bright light into her eyes and ears. Next, he placed a thermometer under her tongue. The results appeared to be satisfactory. Then, the doctor tried to examine Baby Margot. She absolutely refused to open her mouth, but when the light shone into her eyes, she let out a loud wail. Quickly, the doctor pushed down her tongue and peered down her throat. Margot was declared healthy. One by one, the other family members passed through the medical inspection. Amazingly, even Eduard slipped through.

A security guard directed them to the customs officials, where another long line of immigrants waited. At last, Eduard and Frank hoisted their suitcases onto the counter. Livia placed her handbag beside the other baggage. A man snapped open their battered bags and rifled through their clothing. Nodding his head, he slammed the suitcases shut and tagged them with a blue ticket. He pushed Livia's handbag toward her, but heaved the suitcases unto a wooden cart. "Next, please," he shouted. Dagmar's face flushed. She was carrying the cardboard box of 'Knorr's Pea Sausage', tied up with string. What would the custom's official think when he opened it to find Margot's potty? For some unknown reason, he waved Dagmar on, totally ignoring the box.

Now, that the whole family had passed through customs, they expected to get their suitcases back. Instead, they saw the wagon, loaded with their precious belongings, being pulled to wire cages at the back of the reception hall. There, a porter grabbed each piece of baggage and deposited it behind bars. Livia spotted their bundle of bedding and their crates already inside the cage. Was Canada like Communist East Germany, where your possessions could be seized at random? Livia's head spun and she collapsed onto a wooden bench.

"Are you sick, Mommy?" Dagmar inquired anxiously and flopped down beside her mother.

"What is happening to our belongings?" Livia gasped. She clutched Margot's body so tightly that the child whimpered. No one was going to take her baby away!

Frank, who had learned some English in Germany, approached the security guard. "Please sir," he inquired. "They took away all our things."

"Don't worry," the man replied. "You will get them back. We are only storing them in that cage until you board the train." Frank returned to his family with a smile. After he had reassured his mother, she started to feel a little better.

Soon, another guard directed the group to the immigration area on the second floor. Clutching their passports and important documents, they squirmed restlessly on wooden benches. At last, they were summoned to the counter. The official examined their papers carefully. Then, he pounded a stamp on five yellow cards and handed them to Eduard. Each card bore a valuable inscription, 'Landed Immigrant.' Proudly, each member of the Falk family clung to this magic key to Canada.

With their initial trials over, they pushed their way to the train ticket counter. Eduard laid their papers before the official. Frank, acting as the interpreter, stood by. "Our tickets, we need our tickets," Frank pleaded.

The agent slowly ran his finger down a long list. He frowned and looked up. "Who was your sponsor to come to Canada?" he asked.

"My Aunt, Gerda Dust, in Winnipeg," answered Frank. "But actually, our fare was pre-paid by the Baptist Church Alliance."

The ticket agent's frown deepened. "I don't have any record of pre-payment for your train fare." He shook his head. "Please wait a moment, while I contact head office."

While the agent was on the telephone, Livia stared bleakly at Eduard. He had a vacant look in his eyes. In a minute, the agent returned to the desk. "I'm very sorry." He spread out his fingers. "I cannot issue any tickets to you. Your train fare has not been paid."

"What will we do now?" Livia's voice shook. Her head was spinning. "Where will we go?"

The ticket agent alerted the security guard nearby. "Take these folks to the detention center," he said. "The people there will know how to deal with this situation."

"Come with me," commanded the guard. He led his stunned followers through the crowd to the far end of the hall. A heavy metal door opened to the detention area and clanged shut behind the new detainees. Stunned, the Falk family stared at the iron bars, which secured the high windows in the hallway.

"Oh my God!" exclaimed Livia. "We are in jail" She threw her hands in front of her face and began to sob. Dagmar grabbed her little sister's hand and tried to blink away the tears in her own eyes. Frank cast his eyes to the floor, wishing a hole would open to swallow him up. Eduard stood rooted to the spot. For once, all words had left him.

"Hush, hush, my dear." A woman placed her arm around Livia's shaking shoulders. "We will look after you." She led the family into the sitting room. Sighing loudly, the exhausted mother dropped into a soft armchair. Eduard and the children plopped onto the couch. Haltingly, Frank explained their plight to the matron.

"Please don't worry about anything," the woman assured the family. "We will send a telegram to Winnipeg, immediately. I am sure that your problem will be cleared up in a short time." After Frank had translated the message, Livia dabbed her eyes and gradually stopped sniffling. "In the meantime," continued the matron. "We have to separate your family. Your husband and son will be staying in the men's quarters. I will take you and your daughters to a room in the women's quarters. Please follow me." The matron beckoned to the mother and her daughters.

Still in a daze, Livia took Margot's hand and followed the woman. Dagmar trailed along behind, still carrying the vital box. A few steps brought them to a small room. Two sets of bunk beds lined the walls and beneath a barred window stood a small table and two wooden chairs. On one of the beds, sat a young, dark haired woman with a child in her arms.

"Please meet Mrs. Louisa Lorretti from Italy and her daughter, Rosa." The Matron extended her hand to Louisa. "Because we are short of space, you will have to share this room. Louisa, Please meet Mrs. Falk and her daughters, Dagmar and Margot." The newcomers smiled and nodded their heads.

When the matron had left, Livia surveyed their new accommodations more closely. She was glad that the room looked clean. On each of the empty bunk beds lay a rolled up blanket and a pillow. A loud knock sounded on the door and another worker poked her head inside. "Here are sheets for your beds and towels and soap for the washroom," she said. She handed the bundle over and disappeared. Quickly, Livia started to make their beds. Dagmar would have to sleep on the top bunk, while she and Margot would share the bottom one.

While the newcomer was busy, Louisa watched with big eyes. When the job was finished, Livia plopped onto the other chair and smiled at her fellow 'prisoner.' Louisa smiled back. "Bambino—very seek," the little lady pointed to her daughter. "Ees very seek on sheep." Livia nodded. She could see scabs on little Rosa's body. "Papa ees in Toronto. Ve go der ven Bambino ees goot." Louisa talked with her hands as well as with her lips.

Gradually, Livia understood that the young mother and child had been quarantined. Now that Rosa had recovered from measles, they would be allowed to travel on to Toronto. What a hardship this illness must have been! Perhaps, our situation is not so bad after all, thought Livia.

At noon hour, all the occupants of the detention center were herded into the hallway. A guard counted them and unlocked the door. Then the group marched toward the cafeteria. "This treatment really makes me feel like a prisoner," grumbled Livia, but she determined not to cry any more.

At the cafeteria, each family member took a tray and slid it past the serving counter. Frank screwed up his face when a mound of mush was slapped onto his plate. Livia wrinkled her nose at the unpleasant, sour smell coming from the kitchen. At the table, the family only picked at the tasteless food. Even though they were still hungry, most of the meal remained on their plates. Their supper was not much better. The Falk family had learned not to be fussy, but this food was inedible.

On the following morning, a worker took them aside before they went to the cafeteria. Livia feared that they would be reprimanded for leaving food on their plates. To her surprise, the woman led them out of the building to a restaurant across the street. "Order something that you can eat," the worker said. Oh how the Falk family enjoyed that meal! During the remainder of their stay, they always ate at the restaurant.

By next day, Livia got over the shock of being detained. What was the use of moping around? Instead, she took her girls into the bright sitting room. There, Eduard and Frank joined them. With her lovely alto voice, Livia began to sing a German hymn. Soon, her children joined in. Eduard tried, but only sang in monotone. One hymn followed another. Back in Germany, Livia and the children had memorized one English chorus, which they sang over and over again. The melodies drew the staff members into the sitting room. "How lovely your singing sounds," the matron commented. "Please sing some more!"

On the next day, Livia and her family were again entertaining the other inmates with songs. In the doorway, staff members lingered, listening as the melodies rose and fell. After the singers grew weary, the matron brought little gifts for each of the children. Margot hugged a small doll. Frank immediately started to read the comic book, and Dagmar grinned with delight when she received a scrapbook, pasted full of old greeting cards. She especially liked the ones that puffed out in the middle when opened. With glowing eyes, Livia thanked the staff for their kindness.

On the third day of their detention, the Falk family heard welcome news. The Baptist Alliance in Winnipeg had paid their train fare. All their stored baggage was being loaded. They needed to be ready to leave right after breakfast. This time, everyone rejoiced when the heavy doors of the detention center slammed shut behind them for the last time.

Before long, the family was settled on the passenger coach. The train whistled and the steam engine pulled its snaking tail of cars out of the station. Billows of black smoke drifted into the winter sky. Gradually, the C.N. train wound its way past rows of houses and shops, out of the city of Halifax.

Livia and the children strained to see the landscape that sped past, but Eduard soon fell asleep. On and on, the train rattled along the tracks. Fields covered in glistening snow and trees wearing fluffy, white mantles whizzed past. When the train stopped briefly, the children gawked at the long icicles, hanging like sharp teeth from the eaves at the station. Never had they experienced winter like this in their old home in northern Germany.

The train compartment grew colder as they traveled west. Although the passenger cars were heated by steam from the engine, they were never warm enough. Cold drafts blew from ice-encrusted window ledges. The children tightened their winter coats and snuggled closer together. Occasionally, someone got up to use the washroom.

After they had travelled for hours, breakfast was only a distant memory. How ravenous the children felt! Livia had purchased a little food from the Detention Center canteen before they left. She broke the package open, hoping that it would go a long way. Her five dollars had to last all the way to Winnipeg. Whenever the food vendor passed through their compartment, the mother shook her head. Her children knew better than to plead for a treat.

Darkness descended upon the countryside, but the train rattled on. Livia's body ached from all the bouncing around. Their train fare had not covered the extra cost of berths. They would have to spend the night on the same hard, wooden seats. Groggily, they leaned against one another and swayed back and forth in rhythm with the train. Every time the train stopped at a station, they were jarred awake by squealing brakes. Only Baby Margot slept through the whole night in her mother's arms.

At last, morning dawned. Eduard was so stiff that he could barely move. "Ouch!" he groaned as he stretched. "Everything hurts. I don't know how I can endure the rest of this journey."

"You will just have to grit your teeth and endure it, Eddek," answered Livia. She gave Margot to Dagmar, stood up and stretched. "We are all stiff this morning."

Everyone needed nourishment after the uncomfortable night. Livia spent some of her money to purchase rolls, tea and milk for breakfast. Her family certainly could not afford the luxury of the dining car.

Before noon, the train rumbled into the province of Quebec. The family had to change trains at Montreal. In a short time, they rolled past the outskirts of the large city and into a huge terminal. They grabbed their hand luggage and descended onto the platform. Luckily, the conductor realized that they were confused immigrants and directed them toward the correct train. Porters were already transferring the baggage. The Falk family breathed sighs of relief when they were once more seated on the train destined for Winnipeg.

During the day, the train traveled into Ontario. An endless, white wilderness stretched in every direction, dotted occasionally by small settlements. The train whistle echoed eerily at each crossing. Sometimes, the rails skimmed along the edge of an immense frozen lake. Next, they barely squeezed between huge, snowcapped boulders. 'What a vast, wild country this is! It looks nothing like our old homeland. Perhaps, it is more like Siberia,' thought Livia as she gazed out the window.

On the third day of their journey, the trees, rocks and lakes fell further behind them. Livia and the children gazed at wide-open fields, reaching to the horizon. Across the prairie, gusts of wind swept clouds of snow. On either side of the low-hanging sun, blazed brilliant lights. "Those are sundogs," explained a fellow passenger. "They are formed by ice crystals in the air." The frozen rainbows in the sky dazzled their eyes. How cold it must be outside!

Soon, the conductor entered their car. "We will be arriving in Winnipeg in one hour," he announced. "Be sure to have all your hand baggage ready for departure from the train."

Right on schedule, the train rumbled through the outskirts of Winnipeg, into the heart of the city. It screeched to a stop inside Union Station. Clutching their possessions, the Falk family descended from the train. Porters started unloading crates and bundles from the baggage hold. The two wooden crates with their identification tags landed beside their bedding bundle and suitcases on the dock. Livia, Eduard and the children huddled together close by. Throngs of people milled around them.

Livia scanned the crowd for a familiar face. There she was. "Gerda!" screamed Livia and waved her arms. "We are over here." Gerda shoved her way through the crowd to her relatives. Joyfully, she hugged first Livia and then, the children and Eduard.

"Welcome to Winnipeg," she beamed. "How glad I am to see you! I have hired a taxi to take you to your new home, but those crates and that bundle are much too big to fit in."

"We can't just leave them sitting here." Livia wrinkled her forehead as she stared at the crates. "They contain all our worldly belongings."

"We will place them in temporary storage," answered Gerda and hailed a porter. "Later on today, I will ask friends, who own a truck, to fetch them." Once this urgent business had been cared for, the relatives walked toward the exit.

As they stepped outside, an icy blast nearly took their breath away. Had their quest for fulfillment brought them to the North Pole?

Quickly, Gerda grabbed Livia's arm and led her and the others to the waiting taxi. A thick cloud of exhaust engulfed the family. Coughing and sputtering, they dropped into the warm interior of the taxi. "No. 57, Albert Street," said Gerda to the driver as he sped off.

CHAPTER 2

As the taxi wound its way through the streets, Livia vainly tried to peer through the fogged-up window. The two side windows were covered with transparent shields. At least, Eduard could see something through them. Livia cleared a small spot with her hankie and squinted. At first, tall buildings rushed past. The taxi turned off the main thoroughfare onto a side street, where narrow wooden houses huddled closely together. The brakes squealed as the taxi came to a stop in front of a two-story house.

"Here we are," said Gerda. "This is your new home. She paid the driver and helped her relatives out of the cab. The driver shoved the suitcases over a snow bank, onto the icy sidewalk. Then, he waved, jumped into his vehicle and sped off. Just as the newcomers were about to enter the front door, it flew open and nearly knocked Gerda over. Out stumbled a man, carrying a load of cardboard boxes. Right behind him, came a woman with an overloaded wicker basket in her arms.

"Oh hello!" The man nodded his head at the new family. "Please go in. I'll talk to you in a minute." Dumbfounded, Gerda and her charges stood in the hallway. More boxes and bundles filled a corner. Immediately to the right, a doorway opened to an empty living room.

In a few minutes, the man had deposited his load into his car and returned to the house. His wife followed after him. She gawked at the newcomers and mumbled, "Hello."

The man doffed his fur cap. "Welcome to Winnipeg," he said haltingly in German. "You must be the new family."

"Yes," answered Gerda. "They are my relatives. I rented a suite for them."

"Oh yes," the man rubbed the stubble on his chin. "Now I remember."

Eduard tried to be polite. He pointed first to himself and then, to the others. "I am Eduard Falk and these are my wife and children."

"Your apartment is upstairs," interjected the woman in broken German. "We are moving out today, to another place."

"After we are gone, you may keep the washing machine in the basement," her husband continued. "We bought a new one."

"Well, make yourselves comfortable," the woman said. "We are almost finished."

Gerda was surprised at the unforeseen developments, but she just nodded her head. She had paid these people $30 rent for the upstairs suite so that Eduard, Livia and the children would have a home.

"Come." Gerda motioned with her hand. "Follow me upstairs." At the top of the landing, she unlocked the door. Close behind her, the others crowded into the kitchen/sitting room. A refrigerator, stove and sink hugged the far wall. In the middle of the room, stood a wooden table and four chairs. At the other end, a sagging sofa and chair leaned against the other wall. Livia could hardly imagine how they would all fit into such close quarters. Anxious to see the rest of the suite, the family filed down a narrow hallway. It was flanked by two bedrooms and led directly to a bathroom.

Livia and Eduard stumbled into the larger bedroom. Wearily, they dropped their suitcases. They kept on their winter coats, because they still felt chilled from outside. In the other bedroom, the girls jumped onto the double bed. Frank would have to sleep on the sofa in the sitting room. Eventually, everyone warmed up enough to doff their outer clothing.

Meanwhile, Gerda was rummaging around in the fridge. The kettle on the stove let out a shrill whistle. The aunt poured boiling water into a teapot and set it beside the cups on the table. Then she placed a plateful of sandwiches in the center. She pulled a quart of milk from the fridge and filled three glasses. "Lunch is ready," she called. What enormous appetites everyone had developed!

After the meal, Livia wanted to get settled in their new place. She unpacked their suitcases and hung the clothes in the closet. Later in the afternoon, the wooden crates and the bundle of bedding arrived. Gerda, who had taken the whole day off work, helped out.

Together, the two sisters made beds, and arranged dishes and cooking utensils in the cupboards. While the women were busy, the children ran downstairs and played hide-and-seek in the empty rooms. Eduard didn't know what to do and sat on the easy chair reading his Bible.

By late afternoon, Livia and Gerda were tired. They looked around. Yes, the place seemed more like home. Gerda helped make supper and wash dishes. "I must get home," she said. "Tomorrow, I have to go back to the sewing factory. Sleep well." She grabbed her overcoat and hat and with a quick wave left for her own suite.

Overnight, Jack Frost had painted lacy designs on the windowpanes. Livia blinked her eyes at the bright light that poured into the room. 'I must have slept late,' she thought. The rest of the family was just beginning to stir. When Livia's bare feet hit the cold floor, she shivered and reached for her housecoat. Her breath condensed in small, white puffs. "Brr! It's cold in here," Livia exclaimed as she hurried to the bathroom. The toilet seat felt like a sheet of ice. Livia wrapped her housecoat more tightly around herself and went into the kitchen. It, too, felt like an icebox. She turned on the oven and opened the door. "I wonder what happened to the furnace," she mused.

Reluctantly, Eduard and the children emerged from their warm featherbeds into the frigid room. After hasty visits to the washroom, they hurried into the relatively warm kitchen. Eduard tightened his overcoat around his thin frame. "Why is it so cold in the house?" he wondered.

"The furnace must have quit overnight." Livia frowned. "While I make breakfast, take a look at the furnace."

Eduard returned in a few minutes. "No wonder the furnace stopped working!" He threw his hands into the air. "It is completely out of coal."

"How could those people move out and leave us with no coal?" Livia shook her head. "Eat your breakfast, Eddek," she went on. "Then, you and Frank must go out to buy a sack of coal. Thank goodness, Gerda left us ten dollars."

Frank gulped down a mouthful of oatmeal. "Do we have to go out into that icy weather?" he groaned. "The radio says that the temperature is −36 degrees."

"If you don't go," Livia glared at her son. "It will soon be just as cold in here."

Eduard dressed in his warmest clothes, pulled on his overcoat and hat, wrapped a wool scarf around his neck and turned up his collar. Frank wore his winter coat over a wool sweater and put a cap on his head. They trudged out into the cold in search of fuel. Meanwhile Livia and the girls huddled close to the warm stove.

Hours later, they heard banging on the door downstairs. "Your father and brother are back," Livia said to her daughters and rushed downstairs. When she opened the door, Eduard fell over the threshold, into the hallway. Behind him, came Frank, dragging a heavy sack of coal. Livia could hardly believe her eyes. Her husband had tied his red scarf over his hat and under his chin. His eyelids were nearly frozen shut and his nose was red and dripping. Frank had been too proud to cover his ears. Now, they shone in a ghastly shade of white. He blinked away the tears in his eyes and groaned as he moved his numb fingers.

"You two look like icicles!" exclaimed Livia "Go upstairs and warm up. I will shovel the coal into the stoker." While Livia started the furnace again, the fellows thawed out their frozen limbs. Their frostbitten skin turned bright red and started to burn like fire. What a pathetic sight met Livia, when she came upstairs! Quickly she dug in her first aid kit for a soothing ointment. It helped to ease the stinging and burning sensations.

When Gerda came to visit after work, she gasped. "What happened to Eddek and Frank?" she asked.

"They were badly frostbitten when they went to search for coal," answered Livia. "Our furnace stopped working last night for lack of fuel."

"Oh, those scoundrels!" Gerda stamped her foot. "They moved out and left you with no coal?"

"That is true," replied Livia. "Thank God, we have the furnace back on!" Gerda shook her head in dismay. How could local residents take such advantage of new immigrants? Even though Gerda was terribly upset, she tried to reassure her relatives before she went home. "The worst is over," she said. "Things will get better from now on."

The next day broke cold, crisp and clear. At least, the apartment felt cozy this morning. At breakfast, Livia looked closely at Eduard. He seemed to have recovered from yesterday. "Eddek, it is high time for you to find a job," Livia said. "We cannot live off Gerda forever."

"What can I do?" Eduard shrugged his shoulders and went on eating his breakfast.

Before Livia could reply, a loud knock rattled the kitchen door. Frank sprang up to open it. In the doorway, stood an officer in uniform. He held out a badge. "Corporal Stephen Brown," the man introduced himself. "Investigator for the Winnipeg Police Service." All eyes riveted on the officer. What did he want from them? Was he going to arrest them? "When did you and your family move into this suite?" The investigator addressed Eduard. The man of the house shrugged his shoulders. Frank answered instead.

"We came here two days ago," he replied in stilted English. "My Aunt Gerda has paid $30 for one month's rent to the people who lived here. They moved out on the day we moved in."

"I see!" The officer scratched his head under his cap. "I am sorry to tell you this, but you will have to leave. This whole house has been rented to someone else." Frank translated this message for the others. Livia stared at the officer open-mouthed.

"You can't just put us out on the street," she exclaimed in German. "My sister paid the rent." Frank translated again.

"The people who took your sister's money are a couple of crooks," explained the policeman. "They had not paid rent on this house for over four months. Then, they even took the $30 and disappeared."

"What shall we do now?" whimpered Livia and slumped onto the kitchen chair. Tears sprang into her eyes and her shoulders started to shake. Taking a cue from her mother, Margot started to howl. Dagmar recognized the telltale signs of another family crisis.

"Please don't cry, Mommy," she pleaded and threw her arms around her mother's neck. Frank picked up his little sister and rocked her gently. Eduard cowered, at a loss for words. The investigator shifted from one foot to another.

"I will give you a few days to find another place," the officer finally conceded. "But, you must be out of here by the middle of February. Good Luck!" with that, he turned on his heels and marched down the stairs.

As soon as the door had closed, Livia jumped up from her chair and pointed her finger at Eduard. "You had better do something about this." Her dark eyes blazed. "Go to see the pastor at the church. He must know someone who can help us." Eduard hung his head, but Liva stormed on. "Do you want to see your wife and children out on the street in the middle of winter?"

"All right! All right!" Eduard shouted. He slowly rose from his armchair. "Where is that city map, so I can find my way?" After Eduard had squinted at the map for a while, he donned his winter coat and once more tied the scarf over his hat. He would have to walk to the church. Frank, who still held his baby sister, snickered at his father's comical appearance.

"How embarrassing!" he whispered to Dagmar. Livia was also embarrassed, but what else could they do? She nearly pushed Eduard out the door.

"Be sure to come back with good news," she yelled after him.

The rest of the morning dragged on. Housework did not take much time in this small place. Because Livia was too restless to sit down and read, she started rummaging through the cupboards, removing anything that they could do without. She dragged the objects downstairs and packed them back into the empty wooden crates. While her mother scurried around, Dagmar amused her little sister with paper dolls cut out of old newspapers. Frank took refuge in the bedroom with a book.

Hours later, Eduard trudged back into the house. He coughed and sputtered for a long time before he could talk. "I have found a place for us," he finally croaked. "The pastor did some calling on the telephone. We can have two rooms in the home of Brother and Sister Kunzel. They will send a truck to help us move in two days."

"Thank the Lord!" cried Livia. "By then, I will have finished packing."

As promised, the truck pulled up on the appointed day. Two burly fellows jumped out and tramped up the stairs. In a short time, they loaded all the suitcases, bundles and crates. Eduard simply looked on, quite thankful that he did not have to carry anything. When the suite was empty, Eduard, Livia and Margot crawled into the backseat of the truck. Frank and Dagmar rode in the covered box at the back, with all the baggage.

The trip into the west end of the city did not take long. Soon, the men carried the baggage upstairs into the Kunzel residence. Then, while the rest of the Falk family climbed up into their new quarters, Eduard thanked the movers. Livia and the children gladly shed their winter coats.

They had barely surveyed their new surroundings, when someone knocked on the door. Livia opened it to a stout, short lady, dressed in a brightly flowered dress. Her gray hair was frizzy and stood up all around her head. "Welcome to my home," she beamed. "I am Hilde Kunzel." She enfolded Livia in a bear hug.

Livia squirmed out of the stranglehold. "Thank you for your hospitality," she said. "We are very grateful to you for taking us in on such short notice."

"Oh, it is the least I can do," replied *Frau* Kunzel. "After all, you are my family in the Lord."

"Allow me to introduce my children, Frank, Dagmar and Margot." Livia pointed to each child in turn. "My husband stayed downstairs to thank the movers."

"These two bedrooms used to be for our children," their hostess explained. "Now, they have grown up and moved away. I am so happy to have these rooms filled again."

"We hope that we will not have to impose on your hospitality for long," Livia said. "As soon as we can, we will find a place of our own."

"In the meantime, make yourselves at home," said *Frau* Kunzel in her sugary tone. "You will have to share the kitchen with me, but I'm sure that we can work out a schedule. Well, I will leave you alone now."

As soon as the woman had left, Livia sank onto the bed. "She seems almost too friendly," she whispered.

Not long after they had settled in, Livia discovered how interested her landlady was in all their affairs. She wanted to know where someone was going, or what Livia was cooking. No place seemed to be safe from Hilde's inquisitive eyes. One day, after Livia and the girls returned from the grocery store, several dresser drawers were slightly open. "I am quite sure that they were closed before we left," mused Livia. When she opened one drawer, she found her undergarments in disarray. In the next drawer, Margot's baby clothes were messed up too. "How dare that nosy woman poke around in our private belongings?" she asked. Dagmar shrugged her shoulders. "I'll fix her," Livia declared.

Before Livia left the house next time, she straightened out the drawers. Underneath a layer of underwear, she set up a mousetrap, ready to snap. Nonchalantly, she and the girls left the house. Sure enough, the dresser drawers were again messed up when they returned, but the mousetrap was gone. When Livia went to the kitchen that evening, she saw a big bandage on Hilde's right index finger. "What happened?" asked Livia innocently.

"Oh, I caught my finger in between the door when it slammed shut," replied the landlady. She was not herself that evening.

"What a liar!" said Dagmar in disgust when they returned to their bedroom.

After this, the pressure was on for Eduard to find work so that the family could move. Occasionally, he preached to a Slavic group and received a small offering. Frank had started doing odd jobs during the day and going to school at night. By this time, Dagmar had also started school. The family desperately needed a permanent residence and a regular income.

Livia was determined that her children would not starve in Canada. If Eduard could not find work, she would. She applied for a job at the sewing factory where Gerda worked. In a short time, she became the breadwinner for the family, while Eduard stayed at home to look after Margot. This was not the life Livia had dreamed of when she decided to come to Canada. When would her situation improve?

CHAPTER 3

After several weeks at the Kunzel residence, Livia was glad when she could finally afford to rent a little house. The small, old building stood at the corner of Maryland Street and Westminster Avenue, diagonally across from the Westminster Cathedral. Gerda decided to give up her suite and move into the little house also. With her financial help, they could meet the monthly payments.

When Livia first saw the house, she was appalled. The outside of the house had not been painted in years and the tiny yard was overgrown with weeds. The veranda sloped precariously away from the front of the house. Over the years, dirt and grime had accumulated inside the place. The paint was peeling off the walls and the woodwork was dingy. Before they could move in, improvements had to be made. The landlord was willing to provide the paint, if they would do the work.

On weekends and after work, everyone except Eduard tackled the chores. While he babysat Margot, Livia, Gerda, Frank and Dagmar exerted themselves. Frank started by swinging the paintbrush, a job he had never done before. With Dagmar's help, Livia scrubbed the kitchen, while Gerda cleaned walls and windows in the bedrooms. After days of backbreaking toil, the house was finally fit for occupation. The yard would simply have to wait.

Now, the house needed furniture. Gerda brought a few pieces from her suite, but they barely filled one corner. Because Livia had a job, she could negotiate time payments at a used furniture store. Beds, a kitchen table and chairs, and a couch were her first extravagant purchases. In time, she hoped to add to these basic pieces.

Melodious church bells pealed out the rhythm for the newcomer's lives. Every quarter hour, the chimes rang from the tower of the cathedral. Deep bells boomed every hour and struck the number of hours. The family living across the street hardly needed a clock. The bells became a familiar, comforting sound.

The corner location of the house had other advantages. Bus stops and the streetcar were close by, so that Livia and Gerda could easily get to work. On Sundays, they could ride to church. Stores were located within walking distance.

Shortly after her arrival in Winnipeg, Dagmar had started school. She was put into a special class to learn English. For the first three weeks, she enjoyed going there, until one day. When Livia came home from work, she found Dagmar lying face down on the bed and sobbing.

"What is wrong?" her mother asked.

"Something awful happened at school today," Dagmar mumbled between sobs.

Livia sat down beside her daughter and stroked her hair. "Please tell me about it," she said in a soothing tone.

Dagmar sat up and rubbed her eyes with her fists. "At recess this afternoon," she stammered. "A German boy from our class stole a wallet. When our teacher found out, he flew into a rage. He accused all us German children of being criminals." Dagmar choked up again.

"Calm down, please." The mother kept on stroking Dagmar's hair. "Tell me what he said."

"Mr. Grundy accused our fathers of being a bunch of ex-Nazis. He said that the Germans had caused the war, and now, we were nothing but trouble," Dagmar finally blurted out. "I could not listen to his unjust words, so I put up my hand and asked to say something."

"Really!" exclaimed Livia. "What did you say?"

"I told Mr. Grundy that my father never was a Nazi, and that not all Germans were bad people." Dagmar's eyes blazed as she related the incident. "I said that Mr. Grundy himself would have had to obey the authorities, if he had been living in Germany at the time. It was obey or die, I insisted."

"And what did your teacher say to that?" questioned her mother.

"He turned pale and mumbled something that I couldn't understand," answered Dagmar. "He ignored me for the rest of the afternoon. I think he really hates me." She started to sniffle again.

"Don't cry, Dagmar," Livia comforted her child. "You did the right thing. Let us hope that Mr. Grundy treats you properly from now on."

Dagmar did not spend much longer in that class. After that unpleasant incident, the teacher wanted to cover up his blunder. Obviously, Dagmar knew enough English. In a few days, she was promoted to a regular classroom.

Bias against Germans and other so-called DP's (displaced people) was rampant in the early 1950's. Frank and Dagmar were determined to become fluent in English as soon as possible. They refused to reveal their German ancestry and wanted to blend into Canadian society. Livia had less exposure to English, but she tried to learn by studying the newspaper every night. When it came to official business, Dagmar had to act as interpreter for her mother.

Meanwhile, the family still struggled against economic difficulties. Livia's income was barely enough to meet the most basic necessities. Eduard's contribution from offerings was minimal. His wife pressured him to get another job. From friends, she learned about an opening for a night watchman at an industrial plant. The opportunity seemed to be ideal. While Livia worked during the day, Eduard could still look after Margot. He could sleep when the child was napping and also, right after supper.

Full of bluster over his new, important position, Eduard began his duties. He managed quite well for the first two nights. Before leaving for work on the third night, he had lost his bravado. "I did not get enough sleep today," he complained. "My rheumatism is really bothering me too."

"Keep walking around the building every hour to check all the doors," advised Livia. "Moving around will help you stay awake. You know how badly we need the income." Groaning loudly, Eduard limped away to work. Only a week later, he came home with a pink slip. Someone had caught him sleeping on the job.

"How could you be so careless?" Livia ranted.

"I was very tired." Eduard tried to excuse himself. "Margot kept me awake during the day."

"Don't blame Margot for your laziness," Livia shouted. "You had a long nap just before going to work. What kind of a husband and father are you? Your wife has to provide for the family."

Eduard's veins stood out on his forehead. His voice rose to a deafening pitch. "You have no idea how much I suffer!" He yelled. "No one has any pity on me."

Livia's anger turned to tears. She clutched her bosom. Rapid heartbeats sent waves of pain through her chest. She slumped onto the couch.

"Mommy!" cried Dagmar. "What's wrong?"

"Quick, call a doctor," gasped Livia. "Then, bring me those heart drops from Germany." After Livia had placed a few drops under her tongue, her pain subsided a little. Eduard had retreated into the kitchen, slamming the door behind him.

When the doctor arrived, Dagmar led him to her mother. He felt Livia's pulse and listened to her heartbeat with his stethoscope. "Mrs. Falk," he said gently. "You have angina. Have you had these symptoms before?" Dagmar translated his words.

"Yes, in Germany," whispered Livia. "But not this bad."

"I will prescribe nitroglycerine pills for you," the doctor said. "But you must take it easy and avoid getting upset."

"Thank you, doctor," whispered Livia. How thankful she was for the insurance from her work, which covered the medical expenses!

After the doctor had gone, Livia breathed heavily. "Run to the drugstore and get the pills." Her voice was so weak that Dagmar barely heard the words. She took some money from her mother's purse and hurried to the drugstore. Within a short time, she was back with the prescription. After Livia had placed a tiny pill under her tongue, her pain eased and she fell into a deep sleep. Dagmar covered her mother with a blanket and watched over her for the rest of the day.

This latest episode reminded Livia that her marriage to Eduard was a disaster. She was too proud to admit the truth to anyone. Her children would not suffer from the disgrace of a broken marriage. Livia clenched her teeth. She would do whatever was necessary to hold the family together. None of the other church members would suspect what went on at home.

Because she felt that her husband was a hopeless case, Livia poured all her efforts into her children. Their success in life would be her road to fulfillment. The mother had very high expectations. "You must always strive to do your best," she told her offspring. "In Canada, you can get a good education. If you work hard, you can become respected citizens of this country." Livia insisted on good manners and polite behavior at all times. Her offspring had to be model children, always dressed spotlessly.

Above all, Livia wanted to raise her children with good spiritual and moral values. Faith in God should be at the center of their lives. She encouraged her young ones to attend church. Frank did so reluctantly. He was ashamed of his father, whom he considered to be a hypocrite. Besides, Frank had learned to think for himself and did not swallow everything that came from the pulpit. Concern over her offspring gave Livia many reasons to spend time in prayer.

Amid the physical and emotional distress, a unique sign became a symbol of hope. Near the corner of Maryland Street and Portage Avenue the 'White Rose Oil' sign loomed, high above other buildings. Livia and Dagmar first spotted it one dark winter night, on their way home. Series of lights started to glow, first as a tiny white bud, which gradually grew and grew into a full-blown rose. Then, all went black. Once again, the magic rose blossomed in the darkness. Over and over again, the process was repeated. Livia watched, transfixed. Yes, her life could also blossom in the emotional night. No matter how many set—backs came across her path, she and her children would bloom and flourish in Canada.

CHAPTER 4

How delighted Livia felt when the harsh Manitoba winter yielded to spring! Mounds of dirty snow sagged into pools of melt-water. Strong winds scattered bits of paper and grit before the street cleaner swept everything away. As the sunshine grew stronger, the city donned its spring finery. Feathery, green buds burst open on the trees and delicate pastel blossoms adorned the bushes. New life surged all around.

The winter-weary residents of the Falk home could hardly wait to get outside. They were eager to explore their new neighborhood. On a warm, sunny Sunday afternoon, everyone, except Eduard decided to go for an outing. After they had bundled little Margot into a stroller, the group set off for a walk to the Legislative Buildings. Livia pushed the stroller, Gerda took Dagmar's hand and walked alongside, but Frank hurried ahead, pointing his camera at interesting views that he wanted to capture on film.

Even though the women had seen many beautiful buildings in Europe, they were impressed by the architectural design of Manitoba's Legislative Building. A series of steps led up to the soaring white columns, which fronted the huge edifice. The building itself was constructed of lovely cream-colored stones. The adults and children craned their necks to gaze at the cupola, topped by a golden statue carrying a torch. "That is the Golden Boy," explained Gerda.

"I wonder how he got up there?" asked Dagmar.

"He was sent over from France and then, raised up by a huge crane," informed Frank who had read up on the local history. "The building itself was constructed from limestone quarried at a place called Stonewall."

"Oh," said Dagmar, impressed by her brother's knowledge. Quickly, she ran along the path. A heady, sweet fragrance wafted over from purple and white lilac blossoms. The family group wandered around the grounds, admiring various statues. After a while, they had completely circled the building and arrived back at the entrance.

"Climb up the steps, Dagmar," Frank ordered. " I want to take a picture of you beside one of those columns. His sister scampered up the steps, hugged a column and smiled down at her brother. What a magnificent view she had! On her way down, she noticed a pair of robins flitting about, picking up dry grass and bits of string. She identified the male bird by his red breast.

"Look, Mommy," Dagmar shouted. "The father bird works just as hard as the mother, gathering supplies for their nest."

"After they build their nest and the mother robin lays her eggs, he will bring her food," added Frank. "And when the babies hatch, he will help to feed them, too."

"Wouldn't it be nice if your father could take lessons from those birds," Livia muttered.

"Sh-sh-sh! Livia," cautioned Gerda. "Don't let the children hear you." But, it was too late.

"I already know what a hopeless case my father is," fumed Frank. "Dagmar will find out before long. His remark seemed to take the joy out of such a lovely day. Livia hung her head. After working hard all week in the stuffy sewing factory, she had hoped to escape for a while, but there was no way out.

Gerda glanced at her sister's sad face. She had to do something, fast. At that moment, she heard the faint jingling of a bell. "I think I hear an ice cream vendor," Gerda exclaimed.

"Let's hurry to the corner and I will buy a treat for everyone." Soon, each one was licking a tasty frozen bar and trying to keep it from dripping down the chin. Momentarily, good humor had returned, and they began their homeward walk.

The wooden chair creaked on the old, sloping veranda. Eduard had decided to go outside, after all. His bony frame was huddled under an old blanket, in a shaft of sunlight. He grimaced in pain. Perhaps, the sun's warmth would ease the aching in his joints. He squinted across the street at the forms passing by. Eduard heaved a deep sigh. How miserable and abandoned he felt!

In the soothing warmth of the sun, he dozed and dreamed of long ago. He saw himself as a skinny, twelve-year old, standing beside an open grave. A wooden coffin was slowly lowered into it. His beloved mother lay dead inside it. On Eduard's right hand, stood his husky father, clutching his hat and hanging his head. On the left side, stood his two younger sisters and his little brother. The girls were sniffling, while little Edmund stared wide-eyed. Eduard's own heart seemed to break into a thousand pieces. He jerked himself away from the pitiful scene and found himself sitting on his veranda.

The memory filled Eduard with fresh pain, even after so many years. How different his life might have been if his mother had lived! She had a way of softening his father's violent temper. After she died, Eduard had to assume the care of his younger siblings. Meanwhile, his father became even more impatient. Eduard recalled his father's taunts as though they had happened yesterday. "How did I ever beget a weakling like you?" the old man used to shout. "You are good for nothing, except women's work."

"I can't help it," Eduard had tried to defend himself, but his father's riding whip stung his back. Eduard had gritted his teeth and backed off, but the anger had never left.

Eduard's mind drifted over the years that followed. Somehow, he had been destined for failure. Even though he had completed seminary training, he could never hold on to a preaching position. Physical work was too exhausting. His marriage to Livia had failed. She just did not understand him. His children had no use for him. The more Eduard thought about all the injustices, the angrier he became.

Just then, he saw his family coming down the street and crossing over toward home. They were laughing, talking and slurping on ice cream bars. The children bounded up the stairs, followed by Gerda and Livia. When Frank and Dagmar saw their father, they stared for a moment and darted into the house. Gerda who was carrying Margot in her arms, stopped. "Good to see you enjoying the sunshine, Eddek," she commented and went through the door. Livia tried to dodge past, without talking to him.

"You could at least greet your husband," Eduard bellowed at her. "I can see that you have been enjoying yourself all afternoon, while I am suffering all alone."

"You didn't want to come along, remember," Livia replied in a sullen tone. She scowled at him. "I have every right to have a little fun after working hard all week. After all, I have to provide for the family now, instead of you."

Livia had touched a raw nerve. Eduard's blood rushed into his face. "You have no idea how much I am suffering," he yelled. "All you can do is criticize me." He groaned and slowly rose from his chair.

"If you would only use a little will power, you could do something useful like getting a job," retorted Livia. "But oh no! You prefer to be lazy."

"One of these days you will be sorry!" Eduard shouted even louder and shook his fist at Livia.

Gerda had heard the commotion on the veranda and opened the door. "Eddek! Livia! Stop it! The children and the neighbors can hear you. Come on inside and cool off."

Livia stumbled over the threshold with a handkerchief held to her eyes. She collapsed onto the sofa, sobbing. Eduard limped inside and slinked off to the bedroom. Frank quickly disappeared into his room. While Dagmar knelt down beside her mother, Gerda hugged wide-eyed, little Margot.

"Please bring me the bottle of those nitro pills from the medicine chest," Livia whispered between sobs. Dagmar rushed back with the medicine. Livia slipped a pill under her tongue, leaned back against the cushions and closed her eyes. Her face looked like chalk. Dagmar hovered anxiously beside her mother. After a while Margot whimpered and reached for her mother. When Gerda placed the child beside her, the mother embraced her tightly. "Don't worry," she whispered. "I will get better and take care of my children. Even if your father is useless, you will succeed."

Gerda looked on with sorrow in her eyes. How could a day that had begun so well, end in such misery? Silently, she lifted her heart in prayer for her loved ones.

CHAPTER 5

"Mommy, Mommy," shouted Dagmar. "Look what came in the mail today." She skipped into the house clutching an envelope. "It's a letter from Aunt Lydia and Uncle Bruno." Dagmar handed the letter to her mother.

"I hope it contains the news that we have been waiting to hear," said Livia. She tore open the envelope and began to read aloud.

"Dear Loved Ones,

Thank you for the photos you sent us. The children have grown so much since we last saw them. They look well and happy. We are glad that you are all feeling more settled in Canada.

Now, we are seriously considering joining you in Winnipeg. Because you want us to come, we have started the proceedings for immigration. The Baptist Alliance has approved our application. We still need to get our passports and other documents finalized. If all goes well, we should be ready to sail by December.

In the meantime, we must sell our furniture and many other things. The weight restrictions will allow us to take only basic necessities and a few family keepsakes. Parting from Germany will be difficult for Bruno, who has a good job. We hope he will soon find another one in Winnipeg.

I can hardly wait to see you all again. We will notify you as soon as we know any more information. Until then, we send all our love,

Lydia and Bruno."

A big smile illuminated Livia's face when she finished reading. She folded the letter carefully and slipped it back into the envelope. "How wonderful! I have missed dear Lydia and Bruno so much!" she exclaimed. "Before they arrive, we need to find a bigger house. We can't cram any more people into this small place."

Dagmar grabbed Margot's hands and started to dance around the room with her. "Aunt Lydia and Uncle Bruno are coming," she sang and swung her little sister around in a circle.

"Not yet," said Aunt Gerda. "Don't get too excited."

"Don't spoil their joy, Gerda," commented Livia. "They deserve a reason to be happy."

In the next few weeks, Livia went house hunting. Day after day, she inspected rental properties, but found nothing suitable. The only other option was to buy a house, but how? Good friends finally recommended a reliable real estate agent to help out. He had good news for Livia. "With a small down payment, you can buy an older home, as long as you can afford to pay the mortgage," he said.

The kind agent helped Livia to find a three-story home south of Portage Avenue. Over a period of time, Livia and Gerda had saved almost enough. They were thankful to church friends who loaned the remainder for the down payment. If Livia budgeted carefully, she could make the monthly mortgage and utility payments. Gerda offered to help out with the purchase of groceries.

In the fall of 1953, the Falk family moved into their new location and claimed the main floor. Gerda had a room on the second floor, but the rest was reserved for Lydia and Bruno. The top floor could be rented out to help with income.

What excitement gripped the family when moving day arrived! They could hardly wait to get into their own home. Before long, their possessions littered the rooms. After their few pieces of furniture were arranged, empty spaces still needed to be filled, but that would have to wait.

Eduard soon found a reason to complain. "I will have a hard time getting to the washroom on the second floor," he whined. "My rheumatism is giving me so much pain."

"There's another toilet in the basement," Livia replied, "So, you can take your pick."

"How am I going to make it down those narrow stairs?" Eduard groaned.

"Well, you will simply have to manage." Livia was getting annoyed. "Instead of complaining, you should be thankful for a place of our own." She turned away in disgust. She had worked so hard to make this move possible.

After a week, the Falk family felt more settled. Eduard continued to baby sit Margot while his wife went to work. She walked to Portage Ave. and caught a streetcar to the sewing factory. By this time, Frank also had a full-time job. Dagmar walked to school, not far from home. Gradually, the family became acquainted with their neighbors. Many were newcomers to Canada also. Often, they sat on their steps, swapping stories.

During the summer, Livia and the children made frequent outings to City Park. They walked to the streetcar on Portage Ave., and then, traveled almost to the edge of the city. How they enjoyed the freedom and beauty of the open spaces! After walking through the English Gardens, they would visit the Zoo. Dagmar pushed

Margot's stroller to their favorite spot – the monkey cage. While their mother rested on a bench, the children giggled in delight at the antics of those primates. After that, Livia wanted to see the Conservatory. She admired the lush tropical plants and exotic flowers. "What a lovely place this is!" she exclaimed. "I wish I could stay here forever." That wish was too good to be true. Soon, the family boarded the streetcar again for their ride home. At least, Livia felt refreshed, and ready to tackle her many responsibilities once more.

All too soon, the summer faded into fall. On warm Sunday afternoons, Livia and the children went for long walks along Wolseley Ave., to gaze at the stately mansions. They were surrounded by trees and shrubs dressed in colorful fall foliage. Livia wondered who could afford to live in these lovely places—certainly, not immigrants like us. Making her monthly payments was enough of a struggle for Livia, but she was thankful for a home of her own.

As winter approached, anticipation and excitement mounted at the Falk residence. Bruno and Lydia would be arriving near the beginning of December. " We can have Christmas together!" Dagmar whooped. "Can we buy a Christmas tree before they get here?"

"Calm down," said her mother. "You know that we can't afford to buy an expensive tree."

"But we always had a Christmas tree in Germany." Dagmar just could not imagine Christmas without a tree.

"I know," Livia answered in a sad tone. "I have to budget carefully to buy what we absolutely need. I don't know if I will have any extra money to spare."

Gerda had been listening to the exchange. "I will pay for the tree," she put in. "We need to celebrate Christmas properly when Lydia and Bruno get here."

With fresh hope in her heart, Dagmar planned to get ornaments for the tree. She worked extra hard around the house. For doing the dusting each week, Aunt Gerda gave her an allowance of ten cents, which Dagmar carefully hoarded. On Saturday, she walked over to the corner drugstore, clutching her precious dime. She carefully inspected the individually wrapped, Christmas tree ornaments, sparkling inside their cotton cocoons. At last, she chose a golden, glass pinecone. How proud she was when she paid for it! Every Saturday, Dagmar returned to buy another ornament for ten cents. The storeowner had observed how much this immigrant child cherished her glass baubles. On the next Saturday she gave Dagmar another ornament for free. The girl skipped home in delight and hid her new treasures with the other ones. Each week, the kind shop owner added a free one to Dagmar's hoard. Two weeks before Christmas, the tree was finally put up. Dagmar proudly decorated it with her precious ornaments and strands of tinsel.

CHAPTER 6

What anticipation filled the house! Today, the Falk family would welcome Bruno and Lydia to Winnipeg. Dagmar bounced from room to room. "Are we going soon?" she kept on asking.

"In a few minutes," her mother called from the bedroom. "Just as soon as I have bundled Margot into her winter coat. Dagmar put on her own warm coat and pulled her red, stocking toque onto her head. She was getting hot while waiting, and rushed out to the veranda. Impatiently, she shifted from one foot to the other. At last, her mother led Margot out the veranda door. Outside, frost nipped at their cheeks and noses as they walked to Portage Ave. The fresh snow crunched under each footstep.

Today, the streetcar ride seemed endless. Finally, they got off at the corner of Portage and Main. While they waited for the red light to turn green, they stamped their feet to stay warm. Then, they quickly crossed over to Union Station. What a throng of people jammed the hall! Livia craned her neck and peered around the crowd for any sign of her relatives. In the distance, she spotted a white handkerchief waving.

"They are over there," Livia shouted above the tumult. She gripped her daughters' hands. " Stay close to me. I don't want to lose you." Livia elbowed her way through the crowd to the white handkerchief. She struggled past the last obstruction and saw Lydia and Bruno standing beside their luggage. In the blink of an eye, the sisters flew into each other's arms and hugged, in a tight embrace. Tears trickled down their cheeks. Uncle Bruno gathered the girls into his arms.

At last, Livia squirmed out of her sister's arms and wiped her eyes. Bruno lowered his nieces and grabbed the two suitcases beside him. Lydia clutched her handbag and another suitcase. "Come and follow me," said Livia and pointed to the exit. "I have reserved a taxi to take us home. Later on, a friend will pick up your shipping crates."

Livia motioned to a nearby porter, who handed her a baggage claim ticket.

By now, the crowd had thinned out. Without any interference, the group quickly stepped out into the frosty December air. A cloud of exhaust billowed from the cab waiting at the curb. As soon as they were all aboard, it sped away toward the west end of town.

That evening, Livia and Gerda hosted a family supper in celebration of their relatives' safe arrival. How excited the whole family was! A constant babble of voices resounded around the dining room table. "How was your ocean voyage?" Gerda wanted to know.

"Did you have any problems getting through customs?" Asked Livia. Lydia and Bruno could hardly eat their food. "Let's leave the rest of our questions for another time," Livia said at last.

"We would like to tell you more, but we are extremely tired from our long journey, " replied Lydia. "All we need is a good night's rest." And so, the welcoming party ended.

The next day, Dagmar and Margot watched curiously while Aunt Lydia and Uncle Bruno unpacked their crates. Margot squealed with delight at the spinning top she received, while Dagmar hugged a new doll from Germany. When Frank got his photo album, he was very pleased. It seemed as if Christmas had come early.

This year, Christmas Eve was extra special. Instead of white bread cubes with poppy seed, soaked in milk, the family feasted on turkey. After supper, they gathered around the tree to read the story of the first Christmas from the Bible and to sing German Christmas songs. Even Eduard stopped complaining and joined the festivities. How good it was to have the family together again!

After the holidays were over, reality set in. Bruno needed to find work. Day after day, he trudged about in the cold, but came back disappointed. "So many others are applying for jobs," he complained. "They don't want to hire me because I don't speak English."

Meanwhile, Lydia had better luck. She started to work at the same sewing factory where Gerda and Livia were already employed. When months passed and Bruno still had no work, he grew very discouraged. "Why did I leave my good position in Germany?" he grumbled. "We cannot go on living off Lydia's income alone." As a traditional European male, he wanted to support his wife, and not the other way around. At last, a German-speaking Mennonite hired Bruno to work as a machinist. In a short time, the employer was pleased that he had such a competent worker.

The coming of spring brought a revival in nature and romantic stirrings. Long ago, Gerda had realized that her former fiancée must have perished in the war. Now, she was in her mid-forties and did not want to spend the rest of her days alone. She answered an ad in a German newspaper and started corresponding with a bachelor living in Port Arthur, Ont. One day she rushed into the kitchen, clutching a letter. "He wants to come for a visit," she panted.

"Who wants to come for a visit?" quizzed Livia from her sink full of dishes.

"The man with whom I have been corresponding," stammered Gerda. His name is Otto Streich, and he wants to meet me."

"Well, that is exciting news!" answered Livia. "When does he want to come?"

"As soon as I can arrange a place for him to stay," answered Gerda. "I think I will ask my friends Wanda and Herbert if he can stay at their house."

"We shall look forward to meeting Otto," replied Livia.

When Dagmar heard about the up-coming visit, she could hardly contain herself. "Aunt Gerda has a boyfriend," she whispered to Margot. Dagmar didn't dare say that out loud.

One sunny afternoon in June, Otto Streich arrived in his little green Volkswagen. Dagmar peered through the lace curtains, expecting to see a handsome, young fellow. Instead, a balding, middle-aged man climbed the veranda steps and rang the bell.

"Please answer the door, Dagmar," begged Aunt Gerda. She was unusually flustered—touching her hair and straightening her dress. Obediently, Dagmar opened the door.

"Please come in," she said politely. "Aunt Gerda will be with you in a moment." Then, Gerda emerged, with a flushed face, and greeted her visitor. Rather than face the rest of the family, they decided to go for a ride in Otto's car. After they had left, Dagmar peeked out of the windows again and again.

"When are they coming back," she wondered.

Later that afternoon, Gerda returned wearing a big smile, but not saying a word. She spent most of that week—end with Otto. Dagmar was nearly bursting with curiosity. "Did you see how he looks at Aunt Gerda?" she asked her mother. "I think they are in love."

"Don't be so nosey! We will know soon enough," cautioned Livia. " And don't say anything to Aunt Gerda."

After a few days, Otto had to leave, but the letters kept flying back and forth. By the end of the summer, he came for another visit. Aunt Gerda was very secretive, until the last day. When she returned with Otto that evening, he had his arm around her. A ring flashed on Gerda's finger. "We are planning to get married in early September," she announced. Congratulations poured in from everyone. A wedding—how exciting!

On a warm September day, the marriage of Otto and Gerda took place at the little church, which the extended family had attended ever since their arrival in Winnipeg. Dagmar was disappointed that Aunt Gerda was not wearing a white gown. Instead, the bride was dressed in a two-piece outfit of navy blue lace and carried a small bouquet of red roses on her white Bible. The groom wore a dark suit, with a rose in his lapel.

After the ceremony, a small reception was held in the church basement for the family and a few close friends. Everyone stood on the church steps and waved good-bye when the newly-weds got into their little 'Beetle'. "Best wishes!" they shouted as the car sped away.

CHAPTER 7

Dust motes swirled in the shaft of sunlight filtering through the dirty windowpane. Momentarily, Livia's dark hair glowed in a golden halo. Then, she bowed her head again, over her sewing machine. Beads of sweat dotted her forehead, pooled and trickled into her eyes. She wiped them with the back of her hand, and quickly pushed another trouser pocket under the presser foot. Whirr, whirr, buzzed the machine. One pocket after another zoomed through. Slowly, the hands of the clock crept toward twelve and a buzzer sounded. It was time for the lunch break.

Livia stopped her machine, arched her back and rotated her stiff shoulders. She peeled her sticky cover-all from the back of her chair when she got up. Her stomach rumbled with hunger. On the way to the washroom, she met her sister, Lydia. "Whew! How hot it feels in here today!" exclaimed Lydia, splashing cold water over her face and arms. "Come over here and cool off like I am doing," she said, as she dabbed her face with a paper towel. "Then, we'll sit near the window to eat our lunch."

After Livia had refreshed herself, they grabbed their brown bag lunches and walked back to their seats. A waft of humid air drifted in from outside. It gave little relief to the stuffy interior of the sewing factory. In spite of the heat, the two sisters were thankful for a break. They opened their thermos bottles and slurped cold tea, before unwrapping their rye bread sandwiches, spread with liverwurst. When they had finished eating, they leaned back and closed their eyes. The half-hour lunch period would pass much too quickly. "Who would have believed this years ago," murmured Livia as her eyes fluttered open.

"Who would have believed what?" quizzed Lydia and stretched.

"That we would be working in a sweat shop owned by Jews," Livia continued. "We, who are offspring of the former 'German Superior Race.'" She chuckled mirthlessly.

"Our fortunes certainly have changed," answered Lydia. "In Poland, we brought food to our Jewish dentist in the Lodz ghetto, and now, a Jewish employer pays us, and we can buy food for ourselves. God has a sense of humor, don't you think?"

"I am grateful for this job, but sometimes I can hardly go on," Livia shook her head sadly. "If life with Eduard were only a little easier . . ."

"I know life is hard for you." Lydia caressed her sister's hand. " Now that I'm here, I will do everything I can to help out."

"Without your help, I would never be able to pay all the bills," Livia whispered, wiping unbidden tears from her eyes. "I must keep on working, even though my heart races on hot days like this."

Lydia's forehead puckered with concern, as she looked more closely at her sister. Purple rings underlined Livia's eyes. "Take it a little slower this afternoon," Lydia advised. " And go home an hour sooner, so that you can get a little rest."

Somehow, Livia struggled through the next few hours. She punched out an hour before closing. On her way home, her eyes closed to the swaying of the streetcar. After she got off at her stop, she plodded along the sidewalk. Her head was spinning. Slowly, she climbed the steps to the veranda and let herself into the front hallway. She was barely inside when she heard Eduard's voice. "Oh good, you are home early," he whined. "I've had such a hard day. All my joints are aching."

Livia slammed the bedroom door behind her to shut out his irritating voice. What did he know about a hard day? She started to peel off her damp clothing. Just then, she glanced over at Margot's crib. Why was the little girl still napping? When Livia looked more closely, she saw that her daughter's face was red and tear-stained. Dried blood caked one tiny nostril. Margot must have cried herself to sleep. What had happened?

Anger surged through Livia. She yanked on her clean cotton shift and stomped into the kitchen. Eduard had his back turned, stirring a pot on the stove. "What happened to Margot?" Livia burst out. "She looks like she's been crying."

"That little girl is far too fussy," complained Eduard. "She won't eat this and she doesn't like that."

"So, what did you do to her?" Livia waved an accusing finger in Eduard's face.

"I barely touched her, and she started to cry!" He tried to cover up.

"You dared to hit our baby! Don't you ever strike that child again," Livia shrieked. "You are a monster, not a father!" Eduard raised his bony fist as if to strike his wife. Livia shook all over, as she backed off. Her heart hammered in her chest.

Just then, the front door creaked open, as Dagmar came home from school. On the veranda, she had already heard her parents arguing. She darted into the kitchen. Her father was going to strike her mother. Dagmar glared at him, "Don't you dare do that," she shouted. She grabbed her mother's arm and tugged. "Come on out of here," Dagmar pleaded and pulled until Livia staggered into the living room. With a huge sigh, she collapsed onto the couch. "Shall I get you a drink of water?" Dagmar peered anxiously into her mother's blotched face.

"Yes, please," whispered Livia. "And bring the bottle of nitro pills, too." After Livia had gulped down the water, she leaned back on a pillow and let the pill dissolve under her tongue. Dagmar settled her mother more comfortably and then, went to check on her little sister.

Margot was wide-awake by now and reached out her arms to be picked up. Dagmar took her little sister upstairs to the washroom and made sure that she did her little job on the toilet. Then, Dagmar gently washed the tearstains from Margot's face. The two sisters bounced down the stairs, and ran outside so that their mother could rest. In the Falk home, relief from domestic tension was only temporary.

Livia's main refuge was her faith in God. How she looked forward to the church service on Sunday morning! These days, Eduard rarely made it out to church. From her pew, Livia gazed up at the painting above the altar. In the Garden of Gethsemane, Jesus had prayed desperately as He endured great agony of soul. Livia believed that He understood her anguish. Peace washed over Livia's heart as the organ pealed and the choir sang a familiar hymn. She leaned against the back of the pew and drank in the pastor's comforting sermon. How Livia longed to retain this peace of mind!

As time went on, Eduard's physical condition grew worse. With increasing ailments, his temper became even more violent. Only when he spent weeks in the hospital was a measure of quiet to be found. After he returned home, the tension erupted again. The rest of the family tried to avoid him as much as possible. Sometimes, "Brethren" from the church came to visit Eduard. Then, he loudly voiced his problems. "My wife and children don't understand me," he whined. "No one appreciates how much I have to suffer." How pathetic he looked and sounded!

The visitors tried to comfort the invalid. "Poor Brother Falk." They wagged their heads. "Surely, you will have a great reward in heaven for all your suffering down here."

Livia cringed when she overheard the remarks. She was much too proud to admit her domestic woes to others Instead, she dressed fashionably, held her head high and let people think what they would.

In time, the problems became too difficult to cover up. The children were ashamed of their father's conduct and did not want to associate with him. Eduard spent weeks in the hospital suffering from one illness after another. When he came home, he could barely move, but his temper was even shorter. Clashes between him and Livia became daily occurrences. When Livia trudged home after a long day at work, she never knew what to expect. How much longer could she endure this life? Something had to be done, but what?

CHAPTER 8

A get—together with old friends would be just the tonic that Livia needed. Lydia had decided to throw a housewarming party. After much scrimping and scraping, she and Bruno had saved enough money for a down payment on a little house. Most of their furniture had been bought on time payments. Now, a celebration was in order. Old friends from Poland and Germany had also found new homes in Winnipeg. An evening of fellowship would do wonders to lift everyone's spirits.

Lydia wasted no time making telephone calls and giving invitations. Next Saturday evening was scheduled for the special event. Every night after work, Lydia prepared desserts for the party. She had her German cheesecake and a nut torte waiting in the fridge. Now, she only needed to make her famous strawberry cream torte. She knew that her sister and her old-country friends loved sweets. Only Bruno didn't care for fancy desserts. He would be happy with a jar of "Rollmops" (pickled herring), rye bread, and dill pickles.

Lydia squinted at the recipe in her German cookbook, "Baking is a Pleasure." Sacks of flour and sugar and a carton of eggs still lined the counter. A tantalizing aroma wafted from the sponge cake baking in the stove. Lydia cleared the countertop, and started to chop fresh strawberries for the filling. She glanced at the clock. "Oh no, I had better not burn my cake!" she gasped and quickly, pulled it out of the oven. While the base cooled, she cooked the strawberry filling and set it into the fridge. Then, she beat the whipping cream into fluffy white mounds. After mixing the cream and the strawberry filling she was ready to assemble the torte. Deftly, Lydia sliced the cake crosswise into thirds, spread each layer with strawberry cream, and stacked the layers on top of each other. Then, she covered the whole outside of the torte with strawberry cream. For a final touch, she decorated the top with rosettes of reserved whipped cream and sliced strawberries. Lydia straightened up and stood back. Yes, this cake would be the showpiece on her table.

Only an hour left before tonight's party! Lydia frowned at the clock as she cleaned up the kitchen. She was perspiring heavily and hoped to have time for a quick bath before the guests began to arrive. She had just toweled herself off and rushed into the bedroom when the doorbell rang. "Please go to welcome them, Bruno," she pleaded through a crack of the door. "I need a few more minutes to get dressed."

Bruno took his role as host and greeted the Malienko's, a couple who had also fled out of Lodz at the end of the war. After them, arrived Herr and *Frau* Spatz and the Schweitzer's. Frank, who was driving his first car, dropped off his mother and sisters. He was going out with his own friends for the evening. The doorbell rang as another couple of guests arrived. Soon, the living room was crammed with visitors.

Happy voices greeted each other. "How good to see you, Livia," said Herr Spatz as he pumped Livia's hand. "And how is that husband of yours? I don't see him here."

Livia coughed nervously and forced herself to smile. This topic she had hoped to avoid.

"Eduard is staying home because his arthritis is acting up," she answered. "How are your children doing?"

"Irene, Walter and Andreas are in school, but the boys don't like school very much," answered Gerhardt Spatz.

"I am sorry to hear that," replied Livia. "At least, I can be thankful that Dagmar is doing very well in school. Margot has only started Kindergarten, but I'm sure she will also do well."

The girls went off to play in Aunt Lydia's sunroom, while Livia settled down on the sofa between two of her friends. Ripples of laughter filled the room, as they swapped stories from years ago. After a while, *Frau* Schweitzer suggested that they play games. One of their favorites was charades. What amazing antics these adults devised to illustrate their favorite Bible stories! "Black Magic" was another game that puzzled those who had never before played it. The years seemed to have fallen away, leaving a group of grown-up 'youngsters.' Lydia gazed with delight at her sister. What a good time Livia was having!

The highlight of the evening lay ahead. "Come and sit around the table, now." Lydia addressed the noisy group. "It's time for coffee and cake."

"I don't want to miss the best part," exclaimed Livia, as she led the way into the dining room. The others crowded in behind her. After the blessing had been said over the food, the feast began.

"Your strawberry torte tastes better than ever," commented *Frau* Malienko.

"It is good, but I like your nut torte even better," mumbled her husband, with his mouth full.

"They are all delicious, but my favorite is the cheese cake," said *Frau* Spatz.

Livia just kept on munching and smiling. Indulging in these decadent desserts was simply heavenly. Before long, the coffee pot ran dry and most of the cakes had disappeared. The guests pushed back from the table and sighed contentedly. "What a wonderful evening this has been," said Herr Spatz. "But, we must be on our way home. Thank you, Lydia and Bruno for inviting us." The man took his wife's arm and steered her toward the door. One by one, the visitors took their leave.

After most of the other guests had left, Livia hugged her sister. "Thank you for putting on this party," she whispered. "I haven't enjoyed myself so much in a long time." She gathered up her daughters and waited beside the door. They were getting a ride home with the Malienko's.

When everyone had gone, Lydia dropped into her easy chair. Sudden fatigue overcame her and her eyes closed. She still needed to wash the dishes from the party. Reluctantly, she got up and started her task. At last, her kitchen sparkled. "Come to bed Lydia," Bruno urged. "You need a good rest after tonight."

In her dreams, Lydia was still having a party. She and Livia were gobbling down mountains of desserts. She awoke with a start. The room was dark. No cakes could be seen. "How wonderful it would be if life could be an endless party," she murmured sleepily.

CHAPTER 9

"I've been a Baptist for forty years and I will die a Baptist!" Livia glared at her daughter. "And if you know what is good for you, you will do the same."

"Oh Mom, please try to understand," Dagmar pleaded. "I've had an experience with God in the Pentecostal Church. I can't go back on that."

"They got you worked up. I saw that sort of thing happen back in Poland," Livia countered. "No wonder you think something special happened."

"I know that you find it hard to grasp, but I've decided to join the Pentecostal Church, which Art attends." Dagmar said. " After my experience, my friends at church look down on me, as a 'holy roller'."

"Over my dead body will you leave the Baptist Church," the mother's voice started to quiver. "You are only doing this because you want to hang on to your boyfriend."

"That is not true," Dagmar retorted. "I am old enough to know what I am doing."

"We'll talk no more about it, now," raged her mother. "When our pastor gets here, he'll set you straight."

"Oh no," sighed Dagmar as she went up to her room. "What am I going to say to him?"

Livia could not comprehend what had happened to her daughter, for whom she had held so much hope. Until now, Dagmar had been a dedicated member of the Baptist Church, involved in many activities. Why did Dagmar's so-called experience have to spoil everything? Wasn't it bad enough that Frank had never become a church member? At least, Margot still went to church with her mother. Livia had hoped for fulfillment and prestige through her children. She sank into an armchair and leaned her head against the soft cushion. "Where did I go wrong?" she mused to herself.

Being a Baptist was woven into the very fabric of Livia's life. Back in Poland, her parents had left the Lutheran faith, when they were baptized by immersion, and joined the Baptists. Livia had been grounded and raised in that religious setting. From the time she was baptized at age twelve, Livia had been thoroughly indoctrinated. During their school days in Poland, she and her sisters had stood up for their evangelical beliefs against Roman Catholicism. On religious holidays, they had joined their schoolmates to see the religious procession, but they refused to bow to the icons of the 'Mother of God.' All her life, Livia held strong ties to her Baptist heritage. The Baptist Alliance had even helped her family to come to Canada.

For years, Livia had tried hard to achieve a measure of esteem within the church community in Winnipeg. She had been especially proud of Dagmar's involvement in the youth group, choir and Sunday school. And now – what would people think? Livia's church friends were the only real friends she had.

Livia could hardly wait for her pastor to come. He would know what to say to her mixed-up daughter. Livia knew that this man was not quite as wise as her previous minister, Pastor Sturm. What wonderful sermons that man could preach! Pastor Sturm had often visited and comforted her. He was so empathetic and understanding regarding her situation. Livia had gladly slipped $20 dollars into his hand at the end of a visit. But now, her beloved pastor was gone.

The ringing of the doorbell roused Livia from her musing. Pastor Maertens was standing at the door. She invited him into the living room. After he had been comfortably seated, Livia tried to explain the dilemma. "My daughter has gone crazy, I think," she said. "She believes that she has had a special experience with the Holy Spirit and now, she wants to join the Pentecostal Church."

"Let's hear what your daughter has to say," suggested the pastor.

Although Dagmar tried her best, she could not convince the pastor and her mother that her religious experience was real. The talk became an impasse. The mother was determined to force her daughter to stay in the Baptist denomination. Livia's flood of tears and many pleadings only increased the pain. A deep, long-lasting rift developed between mother and daughter, when Dagmar decided to follow her own convictions.

The situation might have been different if Livia had not been so steeped in her beliefs. To her, membership in the Baptist Church was the ticket to heaven. She desperately wanted her children to stay within the fold. At least once a year, the church held revival services. Then, Livia was stirred up by the fire and brimstone messages. "I am going to fast and pray until your brother gets saved," she had said to Dagmar. "You must join me, because we can't let him go to hell." Of course, Dagmar was concerned, and also prayed fervently. Livia's fasting ended when she attended a social event and a plate of 'Kuchen' was passed around. Dessert had priority over fear.

Confusion about the nature of God clouded Livia's thinking. Sometimes, he seemed like the angry, Old-Testament Deity she had heard of in her youth. If she had indulged her longings for lovely clothes by purchasing a new dress, Livia felt guilty. If a calamity occurred shortly afterwards, she knew the reason. "God is punishing me for buying a dress, which I really didn't need," she said. If one of her children didn't want to listen, she used an awful threat. "God will punish you." Yet, at other times, Livia was convinced of God's love. Heavenly feelings overwhelmed her when strains of beautiful music fell upon her ears, or when the preacher brought a message of God's love. How difficult it was to reconcile the opposing views!

Music was Livia's release amid her many problems. In her youth, she had used her lovely alto voice to harmonize with her sisters. Singing in choirs had been the joy of her life. In the early days in Winnipeg, church choirs gathered once a year to celebrate a "Saengerfest." Choral music filled the ornate surroundings of the old Playhouse Theatre. German and English choirs from the Baptist churches in the district sang beautiful anthems. A brass band electrified the audience with its rousing renditions. The memorable occasion culminated in a mass choir. As the majestic strains of Handel's 'Hallelujah Chorus' rose into the air, every heart was lifted up in worship. Afterwards, Livia almost floated home. How sad that she had to come down to earth again!

Many of Livia's reactions were based upon her religious bias. To her, deeds were either right or wrong, with no gray areas. Modern music certainly fell into the dark area. As a teenager, Margot became interested in popular music. She borrowed rock and roll records from one of her friends. When Livia heard the 'wild' sounds coming from Margot's room she was horrified. She had recently heard a sermon warning the congregation against the evils of rock and roll. Livia would not allow her youngest child to become demon—possessed by listening to the devil's music. She grabbed the telephone. "Lydia, come over right away," she shouted as soon as her sister had picked up the phone. "Margot is listening to devilish music. You must help me to get her away from it."

"Oh no!" answered Lydia. "I will be right over." While Livia waited for her sister to arrive, she shuddered. She could not cope with a rebellious teen-ager. In a few minutes the doorbell rang. By now, Livia could barely gasp out the horrible truth. The two sisters banged on Margot's door. Because the music was turned up, she did not answer right away. Livia banged harder. Every minute that Margot spent listening to that deadly stuff would drag her closer to hell. Finally, the door opened and Margot peeked out in bewilderment.

Her mother marched over to the record player, grabbed the turning arm and pulled it to the side.

"You are scratching my friend's record," Margot shrieked.

"I don't care!" stormed her mother. "You will never listen to such awful music again."

"What is the matter with this music?" Margot asked. Lydia stood back and eyed her niece. She seemed to be quite normal.

"Rock and roll originated with the devil," Livia said. "We were warned against it in church."

"You don't really believe such rubbish," Margot countered. "All my friends are listening to rock and roll."

"What your friends do is not our concern," her mother raged. "We don't want you to become demon-possessed." She grabbed her daughter's arm and started to shake her. "In the name of Jesus, demons be gone!" she shouted.

Tears gushed from Margot's eyes. "Aunt Lydia, do something!" The distraught girl pleaded.

"Livia, please let go of her," Lydia tried to pull Margot away. "You are going overboard." After a tug-of-war, Livia released her daughter. She dropped onto her daughter's bed. Her eyes had a vacant look. Lydia took her sister's arm, raised her up and led her from the room. Livia was clutching her heart.

"Come and lie down," she said gently, as she lowered Livia onto the sofa. "Margot will be fine. Just relax, now." Lydia went to the bathroom and rummaged in the medicine chest until she found the nitro pills. She filled a glass with water and brought everything to her sister. "Please take a drink," Lydia encouraged. "And then put a pill under your tongue. You will feel better, soon." Lydia sat close by until Livia fell asleep. Then, she tiptoed to Margot's room and knocked gently.

"Are you all right?" Aunt Lydia asked when the door opened a crack. "May I come in?" Margot opened the door. Her eyes were red and swollen. Lydia put her arm around her niece. "Your mother means the best," she whispered. "She is concerned about your eternal destiny."

"Why did she have to fly into me like that?" Margot blubbered. "I wasn't doing anything wrong."

"You know how easily your mother is influenced by what she hears over the pulpit," Aunt Lydia tried to explain. "Everything will be fine if you get rid of those records."

"Well, I find the whole business ridiculous!" Margot glared. "In our modern day, she still believes such medieval nonsense."

"Be a good girl, Margot," her aunt pleaded. "Your mother's nerves are fragile and her heart is weak. She is easily carried away."

"I still don't understand what all the fuss is about," Margot frowned. "But for her sake, I will get rid of my 'devilish' music."

CHAPTER 10

How the time had flown! Livia found it hard to believe that her children had grown up. Frank worked on the railway, as a waiter, Dagmar had graduated from Teachers' College and gotten married, and Margot was in high school. How well each one was doing! Livia's heart swelled with pride. With her own hard work, and Lydia's help, she had managed to provide for her family.

Yet, life with Eduard had become a nightmare. His health had deteriorated so much that he could hardly manage. One day, after work, as Livia opened the door, she heard a weak groan. She flung her coat over a chair and rushed into the bedroom. The putrid smell made her gag. Eduard lay sprawled on the floor. A brown stain marred his pants. "I fell on my way to the bathroom," he moaned. "Please help me up."

Livia sucked in her breath. "You are a mess!" she gasped. She yanked open the top dresser drawer and grabbed a hanky. Quickly, she tied it over her nose. "Now, you will have to help me, Eddek," she said as she tried to raise him up. What a struggle she had!

Her husband was so stiff and awkward. Livia pulled and pulled. At last, she dragged his upper body onto the bed. She panted with exhaustion and her heart pounded like a trip hammer. "Now, you must help me," she gasped.

"I can't," Eduard groaned.

"You must stand up," Livia screamed. " I've done all I can do." After much groaning and struggling, Eduard finally got on his feet.

Livia dragged him into the washroom. She recoiled from the task of cleaning him up, but he could not do it himself.

Livia gagged through the whole ordeal. Finally, she dressed him in clean clothes and led him back to bed. She put his soiled clothing into a pail to soak. "I'll clean that up later," she sighed.

Shaking from the exertion, Livia sank onto a chair. Sparks flashed before her eyes. She rubbed her throbbing temples. Eduard needed twenty –four hour supervision and medical care. What could she do? She could not afford the expensive fees at any of the nursing homes in Winnipeg. Hiring someone to look after Eduard was out of the question. Livia's earnings were barely enough to pay bills. She was too proud to ask for help from the church. They shouldn't know how difficult her struggles were. "Lord, please help me to find a way," Livia prayed in desperation. She lay down on the sofa and closed her eyes. Perhaps, the answer would come to her in a dream.

A lush green meadow stretched before the sleeping woman. She skipped barefoot through the tall grass, gathering wild flowers. Ahead, ran her two sisters, carrying baskets overflowing with the mushrooms they had gathered. Light-hearted laughter rippled in the air. Filled with joy, Livia gazed into the blue horizon. Suddenly, a dark cloud started to appear. It grew rapidly, taking on a human face. The sisters stopped running and shivered as they stared at the ominous cloud. The phantom formed a swirling tail, which wrapped itself around Livia. Its powerful force nearly sucked the breath out of her. " Jesus, help me!" screamed Livia.

In a flash the cloud disappeared and bright sunshine enveloped the frightened women. "We must get away from here before that cloud comes back," they agreed. The sisters linked arms and walked toward the road. A wooden signpost loomed before them. "To Medicine Hat" it pointed. "That is the path you must take Livia," said her sisters, and faded out of sight.

With a jerk, Livia sat up. She was no longer in the meadow, or on the path, but back on her sofa. Surely, God had sent that dream in answer to her prayer. What did it mean? The face in that black cloud had resembled Eduard's face. Livia knew only too well that caring for him, while continuing to work was sucking the life out of her. How many heart attacks had she suffered in the last few years? Too many! Her doctor had warned her to avoid stress. No matter what others thought, she must place Eduard in a nursing home. The signpost in her dream had pointed her in the right direction. The Baptist organization had a care home in Medicine Hat.

Before making an application, Livia consulted her sisters. She told Lydia about the dream and wrote a long letter to Gerda. "Go ahead and send in an application," advised Lydia. "Your health is in danger. You can't care for Eduard any longer by yourself." Gerda also sent a quick reply.

> "Dear Livia,
>
> I was very upset after I read your letter. Since I moved away several years ago, I was not aware what troubles you are having with Eduard. First of all, you need to look after yourself. If that means sending Eduard to Medicine Hat, so be it. I hope you will make the right decision, even if it is hard. Please give my love to the children,
>
> Your sister,
> Gerda."

A long, difficult process lay ahead for Livia. She arranged a meeting with the pastor of her church, to discuss the situation. For such a long time, Livia had tried to cover up her domestic problems, but now, the truth had to emerge. Livia twitched nervously in her seat facing Pastor Maertens. As usual, she wore a becoming dress in order to make a good impression. "What can I do for you, Sister Falk," asked the pastor. He was aware that all was not well.

"Pastor, Maertens," Livia began. "As you probably know, my husband has been ill for a long time. He is getting worse all the time, and I cannot look after him any longer. The strain of working at the sewing factory and then, coming home to an incontinent invalid is too much for me. I cannot afford to place him in a local nursing home either. Our Baptist organization has a care home in Medicine Hat. Perhaps, they would take Eduard in?"

"My dear, Sister Falk," replied the pastor. "I sympathize with your difficulties. I know about your own health problems, also. However, I don't know if this request will be granted. Do I understand correctly, that you want the home to take him in for free?"

"Oh Pastor," answered Livia. She twisted a handkerchief in her hands, wet with perspiration. "I am very ashamed to have to ask for help. If I could pay for Eduard's care, I would never be here. After all, he is a minister, and I believe the Baptist organization owes him something."

"Well, if you put it that way," replied the pastor, rubbing his forehead. "Why don't you fill out an application, and I will send along a letter of recommendation." He pulled open several drawers, and then, pushed a piece of paper across the desk. Livia glanced at the sheet and began to fill in the required information. Heaving a big sigh, she handed the sheet back to Pastor Maertens.

"I hope that is all for now," she whispered. "Thank you for you time, Brother Maertens."

"May the Lord grant your request," said the pastor as he escorted Livia to the door.

In the next few weeks, letters flew back and forth between Livia and the care home in Medicine Hat. Medical records and more proof of financial need were required. Finally, after months of anxious waiting, the important news arrived. Eduard was accepted to become a resident. Preparing the patient for the transition proved to be another hurdle. "Why do I have to go so far away from my family?" Eduard whined. "I will probably never see any of you again."

"How much did you concern yourself over the rest of us in the past?" Livia ranted. "Left up to you, we would have all perished by now."

"But I am so sick and now nobody will come to see me," Eduard's voice broke. " I will be all alone."

Livia steeled herself against his whining. She had stayed with him out of pity for too many years. Now, her own health was in jeopardy, and her strength was gone. No longer could she cope with this demanding invalid.

"I wish things could be different," Livia blinked away her own tears. "But you have not been much of a husband or father. They will give you better care in that home than I can give you."

When the day of the final parting came, the children were not even there. Eduard cried and Livia also wiped her eyes. A nurse assisted Eduard into the van waiting at the curb. He would accompany the invalid to his destination. "God be with you," Livia murmured, and turned away. She could not bear this sad parting. Eduard waved feebly from the back seat of the vehicle that was taking him to Medicine Hat.

The specially equipped vehicle transported Eduard directly to the nursing home. A group of staff members were on hand to welcome him. Before long, he was settled in his own room. On his dresser, he placed his wedding picture and a photo of Dagmar with her young family. Then, he gazed mournfully around the room that would be his home from now on.

In spite of the good care he received, Eduard's condition went downhill. How lonely he felt! Once, in his time there, Dagmar, her husband and their children came to visit him. How delighted he was to see them! A staff member entered the room to give the patient his medicine. "Well, how nice to see that the family has finally come for a visit," she said sarcastically. An awkward silence filled the room as Dagmar and her husband looked at each other. "Your mother had a lot of nerve to get rid of her husband like this," the woman continued in a brazen tone.

"Just a minute, please," Dagmar piped up. She could hardly contain her frustration. "Let us step out into the hallway at least. Then, we will talk." The nurse beckoned the couple to follow her into an office. After they sat down, Dagmar glared at the nurse. "Do you have any idea what my mother endured during the years that she cared for my father?" she asked. "Her health has been ruined as a result of all the hardships."

"Oh, I didn't know that," stammered the nurse. "Your father insists that his family neglected him and then, dumped him here."

"Yes, he would say that," replied his daughter. "But the truth is completely the opposite. My mother did the best she could to provide for him and her children. It should have been the other way around. She was unable to pay for his care in Winnipeg, and had no choice but to send him here."

"I am so sorry to hear that." The nurse covered her flushed face with her hands. "I apologize for my outburst."

"I forgive you, because you didn't know any better," Dagmar continued. "My father always blamed his wife and us for his troubles."

"We will do our best to care for him," the nurse went on. "At least, I understand the situation better." With those words, she arose, said good-bye and went out.

Dagmar and Art couldn't do any more for the invalid than to spend half an hour with him. When they left, they sensed that it was the last time they would see him alive. Only a few months afterwards, the family received a telephone call. Eduard had passed away in his sleep.

Livia, Lydia and Margot traveled with Dagmar and her husband to the funeral. Frank refused to come. Long ago, he had blocked out any connection to his father. When the bereaved got closer to their destination, Livia and Lydia started to rehearse the past. Tears flowed as they thought about Eduard. "How I wish that our lives could have been better," Livia wept. "We were never meant to be together."

"Hush, Livia," soothed Lydia. "You did the best you could. For many years you bore the burden of caring for Eduard. At the same time, you raised three wonderful children, all on your own."

"I should never have sent Eduard away." Livia continued to weep.

"What else could you do?" Lydia put a comforting arm around her sister. "Eduard is now at peace, and God knows your heart. Please stop crying, or we will have to worry about you." After a while, Livia's sniffling gradually ceased.

At the nursing home, Livia and the family received the earthly goods, which Eduard had left behind. The few items of clothing were worn out and fit only for the trash. A shoebox contained the remaining personal possessions – a clock, a few photographs, his Bible, and an assortment of odds and ends. It was all the treasure he had been able to pass on.

The funeral service for Eduard Falk was comforting. The presiding minister emphasized God's love and care for those who are bereaved. He assured the relatives that Eduard was no longer in pain in that heavenly home. Afterwards, they all left, with their hearts feeling a little lighter. Perhaps, Livia would be able to enjoy life again when the time of mourning was over.

Chapter 11

Livia peered nervously out of the small, round window at the wing of the airplane. Would this " big bird" truly carry her into the blue sky? She had traveled on wagons, trains, in cars, buses and streetcars, but never on an airplane. Beside her, Lydia was just fastening her seatbelt. The flight attendant walked down the aisle, closing the overhead compartments. Then, she reviewed the directions for use of the oxygen mask, life preserver and other emergency procedures. "I hope we don't have to use any of those," Livia whispered to Lydia.

"I'm sure that our flight will go well," answered Lydia. "We have both been praying before this event, haven't we?"

Livia nodded her head. "How silly of me to be frightened!" she agreed. "After all that we have been through! Just imagine, how wonderful it will be to get away from snow and ice in −30 degree weather to warm sunshine in the tropics."

"We have scrimped and saved for a long time for this vacation, " commented Lydia. "I am looking forward to this adventure."

Her last few words were nearly drowned out as the engines started to roar. With a lurch, the plane taxied down the runway, picking up speed until it glided into the air. Higher and higher it climbed. As Livia peeked out of the window, the houses and cars below became like tiny matchbox toys. After a while, the airplane pierced the clouds and emerged into brilliant sunshine. "Look Lydia," she said, nudging her sister. "The clouds below us look like a fleecy blanket."

"How beautiful it looks up here!" Lydia exclaimed. "The ride is so smooth, even better than riding in a car." Before long, the flight attendant came along with drinks and snacks for the passengers. Later on, she brought hot meals for everyone.

"They certainly take good care of us," commented Livia. "This is an amazing experience!" She was not quite so thrilled later on, when the airplane experienced turbulence. Her stomach lurched as she gripped her armrests with white knuckles.

"Breathe deeply and try to relax," whispered Lydia, knowing how prone her sister was to nausea. Livia took slow, deep breaths, and gradually calmed down. By then, the plane had settled into a smooth flight. Everything went well for the next few hours.

Soon, preparations were made for descent into Honolulu Airport. In a few minutes, the plane bounced a couple of times, and gradually rolled right up to the gate of the terminal. A cheer went up inside the cabin. Livia and Lydia grabbed their hand baggage, nudged their way through the other passengers, down the tunnel, into the air-conditioned concourse of the airport. Inside the hall, they cleared customs and walked toward the baggage carousel. On the way, they noticed a young lady and gentleman waving their hotel sign and carrying bunches of floral wreaths. "They are from our hotel," observed Livia. "Let's go over there and see if they can help us."

"Aloha! Welcome to Hawaii," said the smiling young lady and placed one garland over the neck of each visitor. " My name is Eleini. We are here to assist you." She pointed to her companion. "Julian will help you retrieve your baggage and then we will drive you to the hotel."

How delighted Livia and Lydia were at this wonderful reception! Once all the suitcases had been loaded into the van, they were on their way. Tall palm tees, swaying in the wind and blooming bushes lined the roadway. Occasionally, they caught brief glimpses of the incredibly blue ocean. After ten minutes, the van stopped in front of a fifteen-story hotel. Livia craned her neck to see the top. When she stepped outside, the sweet aroma of blossoms filled her nostrils. She turned and gazed toward the sea. In the distance, loomed magnificent Diamond Head. "This must be paradise!" Livia exclaimed.

Lydia was equally awe-struck. "I hardly imagined Hawaii could be so beautiful," she commented.

Julian asked a porter to bring up their suitcases, while he ushered the two sisters to their room on the sixth floor. Inside stood twin beds, a dresser, a table and two comfortable chairs. A television set and a telephone sat on a long desk, against one wall. The pastel colored room was decorated with lovely paintings of local scenery. A sliding glass door opened to the balcony and to a view of the sea. " Please make yourselves at home," said Julian. "If you need anything, just ring the desk clerk. Have a wonderful vacation."

"Thank you," said Livia as he left the room. Before unpacking, the sisters stepped out onto the balcony. What a sight spread out before them! Rows of recliners, and groups of sunbathers covered the golden sand. Azure blue waves crested into white foam and splashed onto the beach. They could hear children laughing as they frolicked in the sea. Clusters of palm trees and thatch-covered shelters provided shade from the afternoon sun. "Oh, what a gorgeous place! Livia exclaimed. "I can't wait to get out there."

Quickly, the sisters unpacked and hung their clothes in the closet. They donned their sundresses and sandals and took the elevator down to the main floor. For a while, they strolled along the sunny beach. Then, they sat in the shade of the palm trees and gazed out across the waters. A waiter brought them tall glasses of refreshing ice tea. As they sipped, they closed their eyes, and tried to imprint the scenery upon their memory.

"During all those years of hard work, I never dreamed of being in such a place," murmured Lydia. "When Bruno was alive, we enjoyed vacations in Banff and Germany. Those good times seemed to be gone, since he passed away. For the first time in a long time, I feel really happy."

"I wonder if heaven can be more beautiful than this?" mused Livia. "I feel as if I am almost there. All the difficult times I had with Eduard seem like a distant nightmare."

The Aloha Spirit of Waikiki completely enfolded the ladies in the following days. At their all-inclusive resort, they could choose meals at two restaurants or at the poolside deck. Buffet tables abounded with salads, fruit, hot dishes and desserts. Livia and Lydia tried to sample different foods each day. On the evening of the second day, they joined other hotel guests for a beachfront luau. How lovely they looked in their colorful muumuus, decorated with leis!

Red and purple hues tinged the sky as the sun was setting behind the sea. Once darkness descended, tall torches set up in the sand, blazed brightly. Beneath the palms, long boards groaned under a bounty of food. In a pit on the beach, a suckling pig roasted on a spit. The mouthwatering aroma wafted toward the guests. White-coated waiters hurried back and forth bringing cold drinks to the patrons sitting around the tables.

This fantasy—land beckoned to Livia and Lydia. They had read about a magical place such as this in childhood fairy tales. "This almost seems too good to be true," sighed Livia. She inhaled the fragrant night air and gazed around in the flickering torchlight.

"Come, Livia." Lydia took her sisters arm. "Let's sit at this table, where we can look out over the water." The light of the first stars glittered above the dark blue ocean.

After the sisters had claimed their spot, they wound their way past the other tables to the buffet. They piled an array of salads and meats on their plates and started back to their table. Suddenly, Livia stopped in her tracks. Lydia bumped into her from behind. "What's the matter?" she asked.

Livia shook herself and slowly walked on. "I saw someone who looks familiar," she said after they sat down. "I just can't imagine that it could be the same person."

"Who was it?" Lydia said, swallowing a mouthful of food.

"His profile looks like someone I knew many years ago." Livia answered while munching her food. "My eyes must be playing tricks on me. This man probably died long ago."

"Who was it?" Lydia persisted.

"Never mind." Livia tried to divert her sister's attention. "I was only imagining things."

Lydia wanted to pry some more, but just then, a group of hula dancers mounted the outdoor platform. To the music of ukuleles and guitars, they swayed and danced gracefully. Their grass skirts swished in time with the music. While the sisters sipped their drinks, the music and dancing went on and on. The movements captivated both Livia and Lydia and mesmerized them into a dream-like state. At last, when their eyelids began to close, Livia and Lydia decided to go to bed.

In her dreams that night, Livia again saw the profile of the man she had spotted that evening. She knew exactly whom he resembled – Sergei, the man whom she had had once loved. He was reaching out to her and calling her name. Livia sat up in bed with a start. Darkness filled the room. In the next bed, Lydia was snoring softly. Livia got up and went to the washroom. Then, she tried to go back to sleep, but again, the man's image flashed before her eyes. After tossing and turning for a long time, she finally fell asleep.

Next morning, at breakfast, Lydia wondered why her sister looked so sleepy. "Did you have a bad night?" she asked.

"I had trouble falling asleep," answered Livia, not wanting to reveal the real reason. "I'll be fine after I have a little afternoon nap." All day, she scanned the crowd, hoping to see the man of her dreams again, but she had no luck. Finally, she decided the whole thing had been a figment of her imagination.

On the following day, Livia and Lydia boarded a bus for a special excursion to Pearl Harbor. As they were some of the first passengers in line, they took seats near the middle of the bus. From there, they could watch all the other passengers as they entered the bus. Older couples and young folks with children joined the tour. The bus was nearly full, when a gray-haired, bearded man and a plump, red-haired woman sat down across the aisle from the two sisters. Livia sucked in her breath and stared at the man. It couldn't be! It was the same man she had seen at the luau. Even with the beard, and signs of ageing, he reminded her of long-lost Sergei. Livia looked away and wondered what she should do.

When the bus stopped in Pearl Harbor, the tourists followed their guide to the first historical stop. Livia and Lydia walked close behind the mystery man and his companion. After the talk, they lingered for a while at the spot and gradually, walked back to the bus. Livia turned so that she could gaze more closely at the bearded man. She saw his eyebrows furrow as he stared back at her. On the bus, he kept turning around and glancing back at Livia. "What's wrong with that fellow?" asked Lydia. "He keeps on turning around and staring at us."

"Maybe, we remind him of some people he knows," answered Livia, trying to sound nonchalant, but her heart was pounding. By now, she was quite sure this was Sergei. He must have recognized her also.

At every stop that the tour group made, Sergei tried to inch closer to Livia. He seemed to forget all about his female companion, until she protested in Russian. "What is wrong with you today, Sergei,"

Livia overheard her say. "You have been totally ignoring me. This vacation will be awful if you keep that up."

"I'm sorry," murmured Sergei's deep voice. Livia' heart skipped a beat. She would have known that voice anywhere. She wasn't sure if the woman was his wife or not. If Livia could talk to Sergei alone, perhaps, she could find out what had happened over so many years.

When the tour bus returned to the hotel that evening, the passengers went to their rooms before supper. Livia noticed that Sergei and the lady got off on the floor below hers. At supper, she saw the couple again, sitting at a table in the corner. Long after she had gone to bed, Livia still lay, wide—awake. Why had this meeting unnerved her so much? She had been only sixteen when she had fallen in love with Sergei, but too much had happened since then. Sergei had found another woman. Livia was not the same anymore, either. Renewing their relationship was impossible. "Lord, help me to settle down and forget about him," Livia breathed a silent prayer into the darkness. "Even if Sergei and I were able to get together, happiness would not be guaranteed. My life's fulfillment comes only from You." Finally, Livia fell into a deep, dreamless sleep.

In the morning glorious sunshine filled the room and beckoned the sisters to come outside. Today, they were planning to board a sailing ship that would take them on a cruise around the islands. At breakfast, Livia said nothing to Lydia about her inner struggles during the night. Today, she was determined to forget about Sergei and to enjoy the rest of this heavenly vacation. When she got home, she would tell her children about her adventures in Hawaii, but her secret love would go to the grave with her.

CHAPTER 12

Livia pulled aside the drapes from her bedroom window. Dim morning light seeped into the room. Thick snowflakes tumbled from the sky. Livia yawned and stretched, before plodding into the bathroom. She splashed cold water on her face to wake up completely. Then, she washed with nice, warm water. As she did so, she wondered why she had not stayed longer in bed. A long, dreary day lay before her. When Livia returned to her bedroom, she rummaged in her closet. "I need something bright to wear on such a dull morning," she muttered to herself. She tugged at her favorite floral dress. After she had put it on, she combed her hair. She squinted into the mirror. "I don't look too bad for a seventy-three year old—well, almost that age," she mumbled.

Then, Livia walked into her kitchen. She filled a glass with water and swallowed a hand-full of pills. After she had finished her simple breakfast of cereal, toast, and imitation coffee, she washed the few dishes. She would wait before phoning Lydia. Talking to her sister was one of Livia's great pleasures.

Livia returned to her living room and sat down. In this snowstorm, her sister would be reluctant to come for a visit. Perhaps, the weather would clear up later on. What can I do in the meantime? Livia wondered. She turned on the television and flicked from one channel to another. Nothing caught her interest, until she came across a cooking show. The host and his guest were creating desserts made with apples. Livia watched in fascination as they made apple fritters and "Dutch Apple Cake." The last dessert was like the "German Apple Kuchen" she had made years ago. Livia sighed deeply. How she longed for such a treat!

Livia got up and clicked off the cooking show. Her mouth was watering. Doctor's orders were to stay away from decadent desserts. Instead, her doctor had put her on a heart-healthy diet. She realized that she should follow his advice after all the angina and heart attacks she had suffered. In the last few years, Livia had also been battling Parkinson's disease. She found it difficult to control the shaking and weakness. Sometimes, she wondered if she was only a guinea pig for drug experimentation. Livia tried to shake off her worries, and looked out her living room window.

Winter was beautiful when viewed from inside her warm apartment. Pillows of snow covered the balcony railing. White mounds piled up on the roofs below. Thick billows of smoke ascended from snow-topped chimneys. The snow seemed to be falling more lightly, now. While Livia gazed, a shaft of sunlight pierced the clouds and turned the snowflakes into dazzling diamonds. What an amazing sight! Livia turned back into the room. She would call Lydia, now.

In half an hour, the telephone rang. Livia answered it and pressed the buzzer to let Lydia into the apartment block. When she opened the door, her sister was standing there, covered with a light dusting of snow and wearing a red nose. "Come in and warm yourself," said Livia tugging at her sister's arm. "I am so glad that you decided to come over."

"I really had to watch my steps," answered Lydia. "That new snow hides the icy patches on the sidewalk." A shrill whistle from the kettle on the stove interrupted her words. While Lydia took off her coat, Livia poured the boiling water into the teapot. Two china cups and a small plate of Melba toast already waited on the table. Lydia sat down, across from her sister. She laced her fingers around her cup to warm them. "How are you feeling today, Livia?" she asked.

"Not too bad, considering that I have to go into the hospital tomorrow," replied Livia.

"I am planning to accompany you," Lydia went on. "I will feel better once you are properly settled into your room."

"In the last few days, I have been feeling uneasy about this procedure," confessed Livia. "The specialist thinks that the new medication will be a better treatment for my Parkinson's disease. I am not so sure."

"Well, he knows that you have a heart condition," replied Lydia. "I hope that your body will not go into shock when they take you off all your other medications."

"That is exactly what worries me." Livia put her head into her hands for a moment. Then, she looked up again. "I guess they know what they are doing."

"Let's commit this whole thing to the Lord," advised Lydia. The sisters joined hands and prayed that God's will be done.

"No matter what happens," I am in God's hands," Livia murmured, with tears in her eyes. Her anxiety had lifted.

While the two sisters sipped their tea, they chatted about family and friends. How quickly the time passed! Lydia looked up at the clock. "I should go home," she said. "I have a pile of laundry that needs washing."

Livia nodded her head. " I don't know how to thank you for doing my laundry, also," she commented. "I am so shaky and weak, that I couldn't handle it any more."

"I am happy to help out," Lydia answered. "Let me get the dirty clothes from your hamper before I go." Lydia rummaged in the kitchen for an empty garbage bag, which she filled with Livia's clothes and bedding. She put her winter coat back on and grabbed the sack. "I will call a taxi to pick me up at quarter to eight, tomorrow morning," she said. "Then, we will come for you at eight o'clock.

See you then." Lydia gave her sister a final hug and slipped out the door.

Livia went to the living room and sat down on her sofa. She gazed vacantly into space. The room was so quiet that she could hear the ticking of the clock in the kitchen. A wave of loneliness threatened to overwhelm her. Livia would not allow herself to sink into a pit of depression. She got up and paced around the room. What could she do now? Her eyes fell upon a stack of photo albums piled up in the corner. She picked one up and began to leaf through it.

The story of her life stared back at her from the pages. On a sepia colored family photo she saw her image, as a child. How happy she had been in the innocence of childhood! A few pages later, she found her wedding picture. What a wonderful double wedding she and Lydia had celebrated! "In those days, I saw life through rose-colored glasses," Livia whispered. "But it did not turn out like that," The visual record of her married life still made her sad. In spite of all the problems, she had raised three wonderful children. Their faces beamed at her from these pages. Frank had snapped the next photos, during their early years in Canada. Outside the conservatory at City Park, stood the smiling family group. Dagmar and Margot were only young children, then. Where had the time gone?

All afternoon, Livia kept on turning the pages. After a while, she came to Art and Dagmar's wedding picture. Her cheeks flushed in shame. How she wished that she had not been so shortsighted! At the time, she had made such a fuss, when Dagmar left the Baptist church to join her husband's denomination. Yet, Dagmar and Art, who were now living in Brandon, loved her and always treated her well. They had given her four lovely grandchildren. Livia had been so glad to see them all at Christmas. Livia closed the book. The vivid memories had tired her. She decided to take a little nap.

When Livia awoke, daylight was fading. She turned on the lamp beside her sofa. It was too early for supper. She decided to open the last photo album. Wistfully, she gazed at the wedding picture of

Frank and Kathy. She was glad that he had married such a beautiful, young wife. After all the pitfalls that he had experienced, he deserved happiness. At Christmas, Livia had thoroughly enjoyed herself at Frank and Kathy's home. Her only wish was that Frank would surrender his life to the Lord. Livia turned a few more pages. She lingered over a photo of Margot with her little daughter, Melanie. What a sad marriage Margot had gotten into! Livia was glad that it was over. She was proud of her youngest child. In spite of the difficulties, Margot had completed her education and was now a teacher in Fernie, BC. Thank God, Margot and Melanie were doing well! Livia glanced at the remaining pictures of smiling children and grandchildren. What amazing gifts God had given her, to compensate for her own loveless marriage! Before she closed the album, Livia bowed her head in thanksgiving.

The next morning, Livia became a patient in the hospital. Lydia stayed with her as long as possible. Then, the medical team began the process of taking Livia off all her previous medication, before substituting the new drug. The second day, Livia had a violent reaction to the withdrawal. Her body went into shock. Gradually, the medical team got her stabilized. By the next day she was feeling better. When Art came to visit her, she seemed quite cheerful. During the night, she suddenly took a turn for the worse. Although the medical team worked hard to help her, Livia drew her last breath. Her spirit soared straight into the arms of her Savior.

An icy wind scoured the cemetery. It sighed and moaned in the barren trees. Surrounded by piles of snow and dirt, gaped an open grave. Nearby, the family huddled close together, their back turned to the wind. A group of friends joined the mourners. Slowly, Livia's coffin was lowered into the ground. The pastor threw a handful of dirt over the spray of flowers on top. "Dust to dust, and ashes to ashes," he intoned. He opened his Bible. " I am the resurrection and the Life. He that believes in me shall never die." The minister closed the black book. "Let us pray," he said and bowed his head.

Livia's children and grandchildren hardly heard the words he spoke. Their hearts were torn apart by the sudden death of their mother and grandmother. She had been near death's door many times, but this was totally unexpected. They bowed their heads and choked back the tears. Oh how they would miss her!

At this sad moment, her offspring could not fully appreciate the legacy Livia had left to them. It did not consist of material wealth or earthly fame. Livia had given them treasures of much greater value. To each one, she bestowed the gifts that would endure the test of time. Her love had caused Livia to endure and overcome countless hardships for the sake of her children. She had truly laid down her life as a sacrifice. In spite of living with a dysfunctional husband, Livia had embraced life's challenges. Livia's offspring are still learning to surmount obstacles from her example. The legacy of love and faith will go on and on.

TRIBUTE TO LIVIA

Your love – a treasure beyond compare,
Forged in the fire of daily living,
Through self-less devotion, rich and rare,
You blessed us with generous giving.
Your spirit strove on, amid despair,
Fighting the foes that threatened to kill,
With innate wisdom, you chose to dare,
And conquered by force of your will.
Your heart—a stronghold against defeat,
Surging with courage, though physically frail,
In manifold trials, it quivered and beat,
With heaven's help, you did not fail
Your gift – a legacy lavished this day,
Granted to us, our future to nourish,
With gracious hands, you gave it away,
In us, your spirit will flourish.